People Skills
for Public Managers

D1590693

LIBRARY
NSCC, LUNENBURG CAMPUS
75 HIGH ST.
BRIDGEWATER, NS B4V 1Y8 CANADA

People Skills
for Public Managers

Suzanne McCorkle and Stephanie L. Witt

M.E.Sharpe
Armonk, New York
London, England

Copyright © 2014 by M.E. Sharpe, Inc.

All rights reserved. No part of this book may be reproduced in any form
without written permission from the publisher, M.E. Sharpe, Inc.,
80 Business Park Drive, Armonk, New York 10504.

The EuroSlavic fonts used to create this work are © 1986–2014 Payne Loving Trust.
EuroSlavic is available from Linguist's Software, Inc.,
www.linguistsoftware.com, P.O. Box 580, Edmonds, WA 98020-0580 USA

Library of Congress Cataloging-in-Publication Data

McCorkle, Suzanne.
People skills for public managers / by Suzanne McCorkle and Stephanie L. Witt.
    pages cm
Includes bibliographical references and index.
ISBN 978-0-7656-4350-6 (hardcover : alk. paper)—ISBN 978-0-7656-4351-3 (pbk. : alk. paper)
1. Public administration. 2. Interpersonal relations. I. Witt, Stephanie L. II. Title.

JF1351.M363 2014
158.2024′351—dc23   2013038335

Printed in the United States of America

The paper used in this publication meets the minimum requirements of
American National Standard for Information Sciences
Permanence of Paper for Printed Library Materials,
ANSI Z 39.48-1984.

SP (c) 10 9 8 7 6 5 4 3 2 1
SP (p) 10 9 8 7 6 5 4 3 2 1

Contents

Preface   ix

1. Why Public Managers Need People Skills   **3**
The Public Sector Is Unique   3
Networking Across Agencies   5
Change, Mistrust, and Financial Austerity   6
Conflict Is Inevitable   7
Miscommunication Is Costly   8
Culture and Diversity Awareness Is Crucial   8
NASPAA Standards   9
The Federal Executive Service Standards   9

2. Every Effective Manager Is a Good Communicator   **13**
Communication Skills for Public Managers   13
The Fallibility of Message Transfer   18
Leadership and Communication   20
The Dark Side of Positional Authority   21
Case: The New Boss   26

3. Resolving Disputes in the Workplace   **28**
Methods for Resolving Disputes   28
What Causes Workplace Conflict?   29
Case: Flextime   40

4. Mega-Skills for Public Employees   **43**
Listening   43
Asking Questions   46
Conflict Analysis   49
Assessing Cost-Effectiveness of Dispute Resolution   52
Interviews   52
Case: The Redevelopment Project   55

5. Creating and Maintaining Effective Work Relationships   57
Emotional Intelligence and Emotional Labor   58
Motivation and the Public Sector   60
Humane Performance Reviews   65
Interpersonal Communication Competence   69
Demotivators: The Dark Side of Interpersonal
    Communication   73
Case: When Generations Collide   79

**6. Working Together: Meetings, Teams, and Parliamentary
Procedure   82**
Collaborating Across Agencies   82
Types of Group Activities   88
Meeting Management   88
The Specialized Leadership Skill of Building Teams   95
Parliamentary Procedure   98
Case: The Interdepartment Team   102

7. Dealing with Incivility, Bullies, and Difficult People   103
Verbal Aggression and Difficult People   103
Skills to Respond to Workplace Misbehavior   106
Bullying   108
Case: Is the Behavior Problematic?   116
Case: There's Something About Jeremy   118

8. Effective Communication in the Intercultural Workplace   120
Cultural Knowledge and Public Administration   120
The Imperative of Diversity   122
Intercultural Communication Theory   124
Cultural Views of Problem Solving   129
Intercultural Conflict Styles   129
Influences of Culture on Communication   131
Influences of Culture on Management Style   132
Case: Refugees and the Library   133

9. Dynamic Public Speaking   135
Speaking in the Public Sector   135
Matching the Purpose to the Audience   136
Organizing the Message   139

Adding Interest   143
Final Check: Does the Content Meet the Audience's Needs?   143
Speech Delivery   144
Visual Aids and PowerPoint Presentations   147
Introducing Another Speaker   153
Case: Telling the Public to Prepare for Disaster   153

10. Designing Effective Public Input Processes   **155**
Why Seek Input?   155
Bad Behaviors in Public Places   156
Limitations   166
Case: Public Input to Locate the New Bypass   169

11. The Interconnected Web of People Skills   **170**
Nexus 1. Public Managers with People Skills Demonstrate
    Resilience amid Change   170
Nexus 2. Public Managers with People Skills Are Able
    to Separate Listening from Analyzing   171
Nexus 3. Public Managers with People Skills Understand
    the Interests of Others   171
Nexus 4. Public Managers with People Skills Prefer
    Collaboration But Are Able to Make Quick Decisions   172
Nexus 5. Public Managers with People Skills
    Build Relationships   172
Nexus 6. Public Managers with People Skills Are
    Accountable   173
Nexus 7. Public Managers with People Skills Communicate
    Effectively   174
Nexus 8. Public Managers with People Skills Share Power   174
Nexus 9. Public Managers with People Skills Are Persistent   175
Nexus 10. Public Managers with People Skills Embrace
    Continuous Improvement   175

Bibliography   177
Index   189
About the Authors   193

Preface

As faculty members in a public policy and administration program, we knew that there were few resources focused on communication, conflict resolution, and managerial skills set in the public and nonprofit sector context. *People Skills for Public Managers* fills the need for a communication-based, public sector contextualized book. It provides professors and instructors in public administration, political science, and nonprofit management with the tools to integrate vital communication and leadership skills into their courses. Many programs include communication skills in their list of learning outcomes but there is almost no coverage of such skills in typical public administration textbooks. This book helps fill that gap with a focus on applied skills within the public sector context.

The book combines just enough basic theory about communication with specific skill development in areas of immediate interest to those who work in the public sector; for example, interacting with coworkers and the public, managing conflicts, dealing with difficult people, or speaking in public. The book can serve as a standalone text in a course devoted to public sector management or communication, or as a supplemental text for any broader public administration course.

We also believe that *People Skills for Public Managers* will be helpful to governmental and nonprofit training programs that seek to improve the communication and managerial skills of their participants. While it was written with the intention of being used in a classroom setting, the book's applied focus and helpful guidelines and exercises will be useful to individual readers as well. *People Skills for Public Managers* will help readers improve their communication and managerial skills.

Several features of the book make it useful to instructors and readers:

- Adaptation of "people skills" to the public sector and nonprofit sector context including dealing with public interest groups, the constraints of public sector employment, and public hearings.

- An applied focus that centers on helping the reader/student become practiced at the skills covered in the book.
- The combination of perspectives from both communication and public administration.

Specific features of the project include:

- Tables and figures that highlight the steps necessary to master the skills covered in the book; for example, "Responses to Problematic Workplace Behaviors," "Conflict Management Tools in Organizations," or "Characteristics of Successful Interagency Collaboration."
- Case studies to encourage the reader to apply concepts in the public and nonprofit sector.
- An Instructor's Manual that contains guidance on how best to utilize the exercises and case studies in a classroom setting as well as additional exercises.

We hope that readers will find the book useful as they learn to navigate the complex and challenging landscape of public and nonprofit sector organizations. We welcome all comments that readers and instructors may have to help us either improve the book or let us know how the book has helped them in their own experiences as managers.

Acknowledgments

This project is supported by a sabbatical and research funds from the College of Social Sciences and Public Affairs at Boise State University and the department of Public Policy. We also thank our many interviewees in public sector leadership positions who shared their time and insights. Additional thanks go to the research assistant on the project, Ryan McLean, and research colleague Dr. Elizabeth Fredericksen.

People Skills
for Public Managers

1

Why Public Managers Need People Skills

In an era in which the essential functions of government service are sometimes challenged, it is more important than ever for public employees to have good communication skill as well as technical expertise. As Frederickson and Smith (2003) assert: "Much of what is understood to be public management depends upon effective communication" (p. 107). With the public, across agencies, and among coworkers, mastery of the full spectrum of communication skills is critical. Seven reasons impel those who work in the public or nonprofit sector to master people skills: the uniqueness of the public sector; the networking required to complete many tasks; fiscal stress, public distrust, and change; the inevitability of conflict; the cost of ineffective communication; the need for cultural awareness; a mandate from the Network of Schools of Public Policy, Affairs, and Administration (NASPAA), and the inclusion of soft skills in the federal executive standards.

The Public Sector Is Unique

Several characteristics distinguish the public from the private sector and affect how communication occurs in agencies. First, public agencies are subject to numerous laws and administrative rules requiring transparency in government operations. Chief among these are mandates for public hearings, an arena in which effective communication skills are vital.

Compounding the difficulties of turbulent times and a loss of public respect for government are the legal requirements and genuine need to consult public stakeholders about pending decisions. Public meetings occasionally degenerate into unruly invective festivals. Those responsible for engaging the public need a deep toolbox of options if they are to maintain control of meetings and sustain momentum toward solutions.

(Chapter 10 presents strategies for management of public meetings, public participation processes, and public comment options.)

Public agencies in the United States operate within a system of separated powers, which means that agencies are accountable to the chief executive, typically a mayor, governor, or president, as well as to a legislative body that has budget and administrative oversight. This system creates a second unique need for communication skills among public employees. Agencies must be accountable to the taxpayers and policy makers who fund them. Public employees must speak clearly, persuasively, and efficiently when presenting agency budget requests, speaking to legislative committees, or updating officials on a program.

Open meetings and open records laws may dictate that nearly all agency business be conducted in an open forum, giving rise to a third reason for enhanced communication skills among public employees: understanding that agency business and actions will be closely scrutinized by the public. This places even greater responsibility on public managers to communicate effectively, tactfully, and truthfully.

Among other areas, transparency affects public sector communication in the budgeting process. Public sector revenue is dependent on political choices and economic realities. Unlike the private sector, agencies cannot simply decide they will no longer provide a mandated service or start up their own enterprises to provide additional revenue. Political processes inform and control how budgets are set. Balancing direct service and technical program components in an era of budget reductions is a problem with geometrically progressing complexity. For example, Pandey (2010) observed: "the annual time frame for balancing budgets and the panoply of competing goals can have the insidious effect of trading short-term goals at the expense of long-term goals" (p. 567). Agency heads need effective analytical *and* presentational skills so their budget masters can understand the implications of program reductions or mission changes. The ability to communicate well about the impacts of cutbacks may help prepare politicians and the public for service reductions during times of economic austerity. The ability to communicate effectively may also convince elected decision makers to avoid cutbacks to agency programs, or at least understand the probable impact of budget reductions.

Research into the types of people who work in the public arena indicates they have different motivations than those who work in the private sector. Public sector employee motivation may arise from a desire to be helpful to others—to serve the public. This essential way that the public sector employee may differ from those in the private sector deeply affects the options available to supervisors and leaders. Historically, lower pay was acceptable when employees had a guarantee of long-term security in their employment, retirement benefits, and the inner satisfaction of serving the public. Drastic cuts in budgets and the decimation of employee rosters can shatter the compact that was the foundation of public employee motivation. Changes in the general populations' respect for government jobs may impact public service motivation. The final situation unique to the public sector is the need to change management styles as the landscape of what motivates public employees changes. If managers cannot adapt their communication to fit the uniqueness of employees, it will be difficult to motivate a workforce to perform at the highest level of efficiency.

Networking Across Agencies

Modern public administrators must possess the ability to cooperate with other agencies and to communicate effectively across a variety of public and private contexts. It is increasingly rare for an agency to have sole responsibility for developing and administering a project. Problems are too complicated or individual agency mandates too limited. Instead, many projects involve multiple agencies, many times at different levels of government, and may include nonprofits or for-profit corporations as partners. The tools of governance may include networks, contracts with other entities, privatization, quasi-governmental organizations, and grants that entice agencies to undertake new activities (Goldsmith and Eggers 2004; Salamon 2002). For example, a detox center created in Boise, Idaho, to provide services for people with addiction issues includes numerous agencies (see Figure 1.1). Only the combined financial backing and contributed skills of federal, state, county, city, nonprofit, and private sector entities made the project possible.

Networking among and across public and private entities is representative of the enhanced skill set modern employees need. Abel (2009) argued that public affairs students should learn to thrive on chaos, make rapid decisions, and collaborate with teams. A plethora of communication and analytical skills are required to navigate the sophisticated problem-solving environment of the modern era. Those who come to public administration leadership from a science, accounting, or other

Figure 1.1   **Partners in Governance of an Alcohol Treatment Center**

Government	Nonprofits	For-Profit Entities
• City of Boise • City of Meridian • Ada County • State Department of Health and Welfare • Boise City and Ada County Housing Authority • Federal Region IV Health Board • Congressional earmark funding	• St. Alphonsus Regional Medical Center • St. Luke's Regional Medical Center • Terry Reilly Health Services • United Way of Treasure Valley • J. A. and Kathryn Albertson Foundation • Julius C. Jerker Foundation • Wells Fargo Bank Foundation	• Hummel Architects • EKC Construction

technical background may have not been exposed to modern management theory, the nuances of networking, or communication training. An efficient and effective network participant requires both empirical knowledge and people skills. Chief among those skills is the ability to communicate effectively.

Change, Mistrust, and Financial Austerity

Public administrators need effective communication skills to help their agencies and the publics they serve navigate tough financial times. Brehm and Gates (1997) argue that part of the reason citizens hold bureaucrats in such low regard is the combination of fear about the amount of control these individuals have over their lives and concerns about accountability, even though studies show that most bureaucrats act fairly, consistently, and pass accountability scrutiny. During times when uncertainty about the near future abounds, fear impacts the public sector in numerous ways. Economic downturns reduce agency budgets. Job loss and financial fears in the public lead to spirited argument about which programs should wither away and which should prosper. Public employees are anxious about losing their jobs while simultaneously struggling to fill the gaps caused by budget cuts and facing increasing public disdain for "government" work.

Times of change can be exciting, but not necessarily in a positive way. A Pew study found that by almost every conceivable measure, Americans were more critical of their government in 2010 than when last measured. For example, the Environmental Protection Agency's favorable rating fell from 69 percent in 1997 to 57 percent in 2010, with fewer than 50 percent saying the agency does a good job. Eighty percent of respondents distrusted at least one area of government and 50 percent said the federal government negatively impacted their lives. This tide of dissent arose from what was termed a perfect storm of conditions—"a dismal economy, an unhappy public, bitter partisan-based backlash, and epic discontent with Congress and elected officials" (The Pew Research Center 2010).

Times of change necessitate enhanced communication and conflict management skills among public employees and agency leaders. A prominent national leadership development program argues that change management is easier among leaders who have good relationships with employees and upper management (Ruderman, Hannum, Leslie, and Steed 2004). The skill needed during times of change is termed *adaptive work*: "Adaptive work is required when our deeply held beliefs are challenged, when the values that made us successful become less relevant, and when legitimate yet competing perspectives emerge" (Heifetz and Laurie 1997, p. 124). Adaptive work requires leaders who can harness creative ideas at all levels of the organization and who simultaneously think strategically and about critical daily tasks, can help regulate employee distress, manage rates of change, and "have the emotional capacity to tolerate uncertainty, frustration, and pain" (ibid.). While no one skill best relates to change management, development of the array of abilities discussed in this book can enhance the probability of success.

Conflict Is Inevitable

Wishful thinking leads to hope that each workday will be tranquil, creative, and include cordial conversation with coworkers. Inevitably, though, naturally occurring goal differences and problematic employee behaviors lead to conflict. Chapter 3 explains that while it is impossible to escape interpersonal conflict completely, it is possible to manage many interpersonal conflicts so discord stays within acceptable boundaries.

The inevitability of conflict in the workplace is compounded for public employees. Public sector employees are the custodians tasked with managing so-called wicked problems on behalf of the public. These wicked problems are ill-defined, virtually irresolvable, or laden with competing goals from multiple stakeholders (Rittel and Webber 1973). A robust literature in public administration journals recommends collaborative and creative processes to manage thorny issues (see Weber and Khademian 2008). Wicked problems are so widespread that the U.S. Department of the Interior issued a technical memorandum with several alternative approaches to guide collaborative work surrounding difficult issues (Ruell, Burkardt, and Clark 2010).

Miscommunication Is Costly

Miscommunication can be costly in every way imaginable. Inefficiency from poor understanding of mission and duties may waste taxpayer dollars and a misunderstanding when transferring files between social workers could lead to suffering or death. Conflicts left to fester can result in expensive litigation. Effective communication and conflict resolution techniques can save agencies from expensive lawsuits. When conflict abounds in an agency, employees may leave, and it becomes increasingly difficult to entice quality applicants into the hornet's nest. The conflict literature is replete with examples of poor communication and its deleterious or disastrous effects (see McCorkle and Reese 2010).

The need for competent communication is important for all agencies, but it is critical in small or geographically isolated departments. Hays and Sowa (2010) report that many small town and rural area offices have no dedicated human resources officers to help with difficult situations. Employees in regional offices of larger agencies may likewise be isolated.

> **Factoid:**   49 percent of respondents in an October 2010 *Washington Post* poll felt federal employees worked less hard than private employees and 75 percent believed they were paid more than private sector employees.

Culture and Diversity Awareness Is Crucial

A 2011 executive order argued that increasing the diversity of the nation's workforce is both a commendable goal rooted in the value of equal opportunity and a necessity as national demographics change (The White House 2011a, 2011b). Anticipating the cultural dimensions to communication that help and/or hinder understanding between supervisors and employees or employees and citizens is critical. Both public and private sector leadership require a deep understanding of gender and culture if the increasingly diverse workforce is to be managed effectively (Campbell 2004). Clients and stakeholders also exhibit increasingly complex demographics. (Chapter 8 delves into concepts and skills for diversity management.)

NASPAA Standards

Communication competencies are integral to the federal executive service standards and are essential for accreditation by NASPAA. Standard 5.1 of the Universally Required Competencies specifically cites several abilities including: (1) Leading and managing in public governance, (2) Participating and contributing to the policy process, (3) Analyzing, synthesizing, critically thinking, and solving problems, (4) Making decision, and (5) Communicating and interacting productively with a diverse and changing public.

The Federal Executive Service Standards

Many of the twenty-eight fundamental competencies identified by the U.S. Office of Personnel Management for senior executives highlight communication and leadership skills. While technical, financial, and governance competencies are at the core of the standards, specific communication and people management skills are woven throughout. The box below highlights the leadership and communication skills embedded in the twenty-eight competencies.

Executive Core Competencies, U.S. Office of Personnel Management

The Executive Core Qualifications (ECQs) define the competencies needed to build a federal corporate culture that drives for results, serves customers, and builds successful teams and coalitions within and outside the organization. The ECQs are required for entry to the Senior Executive Service and are used by many departments and agencies in selection, performance management, and leadership development for management and executive positions.

Note: Competencies not as directly related to communication are in italics to distinguish among those that are connected to this book and those that are not.

ECQ 1: Leading Change

Creativity and Innovation:	Develops new insights into situations; questions conventional approaches; encourages new ideas and innovations; designs and implements new or cutting edge programs/processes.
External Awareness:	Understands and keeps up-to-date on local, national, and international policies and trends that affect the organization and shape stakeholders' views; is aware of the organization's impact on the external environment.
Flexibility:	Is open to change and new information; rapidly adapts to new information, changing conditions, or unexpected obstacles.
Resilience:	Deals effectively with pressure; remains optimistic and persistent, even under adversity. Recovers quickly from setbacks.
Strategic Thinking:	Formulates objectives and priorities, and implements plans consistent with the long-term interests of the organization in a global environment. Capitalizes on opportunities and manages risks.
Vision:	Takes a long-term view and builds a shared vision with others; acts as a catalyst for organizational change. Influences others to translate vision into action.

ECQ 2: Leading People

Conflict Management:	Encourages creative tension and differences of opinions. Anticipates and takes steps to prevent counter-productive confrontations. Manages and resolves conflicts and disagreements in a constructive manner.
Leveraging Diversity:	Fosters an inclusive workplace where diversity and individual differences are valued and leveraged to achieve the vision and mission of the organization.

| Developing Others: | Develops the ability of others to perform and contribute to the organization by providing ongoing feedback and by providing opportunities to learn through formal and informal methods. |
| Team Building: | Inspires and fosters team commitment, spirit, pride, and trust. Facilitates cooperation and motivates team members to accomplish group goals. |

ECQ 3: Results Driven

Accountability:	Holds self and others accountable for measurable high-quality, timely, and cost-effective results. Determines objectives, sets priorities, and delegates work. Accepts responsibility for mistakes. Complies with established control systems and rules.
Customer Service:	Anticipates and meets the needs of both internal and external customers. Delivers high-quality products and services; is committed to continuous improvement.
Decisiveness:	Makes well-informed, effective, and timely decisions, even when data are limited or solutions produce unpleasant consequences; perceives the impact and implications of decisions.
Entrepreneurship:	*Positions the organization for future success by identifying new opportunities; builds the organization by developing or improving products or services. Takes calculated risks to accomplish organizational objectives.*
Problem Solving:	Identifies and analyzes problems; weighs relevance and accuracy of information; generates and evaluates alternative solutions; makes recommendations.
Technical Credibility:	*Understands and appropriately applies principles, procedures, requirements, regulations, and policies related to specialized expertise.*

ECQ 4: Business Acumen

Financial Management:
Understands the organization's financial processes. Prepares, justifies, and administers the program budget. Oversees procurement and contracting to achieve desired results. Monitors expenditures and uses cost-benefit thinking to set priorities.

Human Capital Management: Builds and manages workforce based on organizational goals, budget considerations, and staffing needs. Ensures that employees are appropriately recruited, selected, appraised, and rewarded; takes action to address performance problems. Manages a multisector workforce and a variety of work situations.

Technology Management:
Keeps up-to-date on technological developments. Makes effective use of technology to achieve results. Ensures access to and security of technology systems.

ECQ 5: Building Coalitions

Partnering:
Develops networks and builds alliances; collaborates across boundaries to build strategic relationships and achieve common goals.

Political Savvy:
Identifies the internal and external politics that impact the work of the organization. Perceives organizational and political reality and acts accordingly.

Influencing/Negotiating:
Persuades others; builds consensus through give and take; gains cooperation from others to obtain information and accomplish goals.

For current standards, consult the U.S. Office of Personnel Management (2012).

2

Every Effective Manager Is a Good Communicator

Career preparation for public administration professionals often focuses on the technical aspects of doing work for the public—understanding regulations and agency procedures, dissecting the intricate web of public finance, or developing specialized skills for a specific job (budget writing, forestry management, and so forth). Another layer of competence, however, is required of public employees: the ability to work with other people efficiently and effectively. This chapter examines two aspects of working with others: communication skills and leadership.

Communication Skills for Public Managers

Managers' mistaken beliefs about themselves or the communication process can impede the acquisition of important skills. For example, some individuals believe:

- "I see the world as it is."
- "I was just not born to be a good communicator."
- "I always say exactly what I mean."
- "I am a good listener."

This chapter begins with an examination of how the communication process is inexact and may lead to troublesome errors. It explains how the perception process contributes to individual and shared meaning, how social meaning is created, how beliefs about the questions of nature or nurture can lead to attribution errors, and how meanings become altered during the communication process. Leaning about the communication process dispels mistaken beliefs about communication and improves effective communication. Next, the chapter reveals the link between leadership and good communication. Finally, a darker side of positional authority is discussed through several errors made by novice leaders.

The Perception Process

The tri-part perception process (selection, organization, and interpretation) explains how individuals sitting side by side can watch events
unfold and describe what happened in totally differently ways. As people
go through each day, their senses pick up sounds, sights, smells, and
physical sensations. All of these inputs are then organized into something
meaningful to the recipient. Finally, higher order processes are brought
to bear to interpret the stimuli.

The act of perceiving and interpreting stimuli from the outside world
engages a number of entirely natural, biological, or habit-based processes
that can lead to wrong conclusions. It is often difficult to see the world as
it really is. No one can take in all of the stimuli he or she is bombarded
with every second. We live in an information-rich world. A continuous
stream of data is available to the senses—too much to be meaningfully
handled all at once. To cope, humans have developed automatic processes
to select what is important from a virtually infinite mass of stimuli. People
recognize threats immediately, can pick personal names out of the babble
of several conversations, and are able to drill through the chaos of play-
ground noise to single out a child's voice if it changes from pleasure to
pain. When interested in something, humans frequently focus on it and
exclude other stimuli. For example, an office worker can tune out the
extraneous noise from outdoors to concentrate on writing a report. When
involved in a task, an individual can be blind and deaf to the swarm of
competing stimuli. There is some evidence that auto accidents occur not
merely because a driver was talking on a cell phone and not watching
the road, but because his or her mind's attention over-focused on the
conversation. The driver was looking toward the road, but the perception process edited out much of the available stimuli. Conversation was
put in the foreground and driving receded into the background. Hence,
a driver literally could not see a pedestrian stepping into a crosswalk or
a car slowing in the lane ahead.

The ability to focus enables individuals to be productive and to concentrate. As the mind selects what is being attended to, one prefers what is
striking; that is, bold, edged, or with a familiar shape. Many illustrations
of *figure/ground* phenomenon are available. Some people see only peeling
paint on a wall; others see the face of a deity. Figure 2.1 demonstrates
the editing power of perception. When read aloud, some of the content
typically is skipped over; we edit out the repeated words.

Figure 2.1   **Read the Words in the Triangle Aloud**

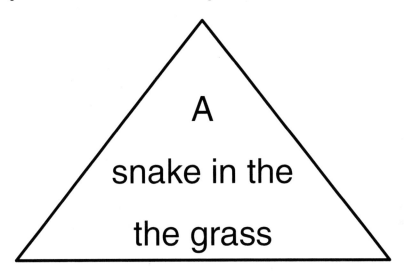

The organizing part of the perception process begins to analyze what the stimuli means. The incoming information is compared to past personal experience. What is perceived and how it is sorted engages highly personalized filtering systems.

During the organizing step, a complete story also starts to emerge from the fragmented pieces of stimuli. People can easily recognize familiar shapes. They also will perceive something as familiar even when it is not. A majority of readers can correctly interpret the word in Figure 2.2, even though it is incomplete. Humans prefer *closure* to fragments, so the mind fills in the missing details. While the preference for closure facilitates the interpretation of incomplete or messy handwriting, it also leads to filling in details about people or tasks that simply are wrong. Asked what a robber looked like, witnesses may reply with whatever is in their personal category of "a robber" rather than the stimulus that was presented to their eyes—so the same robber is described as a man, a woman, black, Hispanic, old, or young.

In the third stage of the perception process a fully formed gestalt of interpretation, with value-laden associations, is created. At the interpretation level, individuals are prone to *attribution errors*, including seeing virtue in a personal behavior and error when others perform the same action—a *self-serving bias*. Attribution errors have been noted in the field of international relations as leaders attribute malicious intentions to other

Figure 2.2   **What Is the Word?**

monument

international actors. It is also relevant to the challenges of developing and implementing effective intergovernmental relations as administrators and elected officials from various levels of government attempt to cooperate. This is sometimes referred to as Miles' Law: Where you stand depends on where you sit (Miles 1978).

McCorkle and Reese (2010) summarize seven ways the perception process affects communication and how we interact with others (Table 2.1). Competent communicators are aware of the frailties of the perception process, work to counteract bias in their perceptual filters, and check the accuracy of their first impressions.

Communication Competence: Nurture or Nature?

"That Sarah, she is just a born communicator!" This comment implies that Sarah communicates well because of some innate capacity—it asserts that the ability to communicate (or not) is more about genetics than about socialization or learning. Notwithstanding physical impediments, scholars generally believe that the ability to communicate is learned. For example, each culture socializes children to prefer certain types of communication. European-Americans continue to prefer male, deeply pitched voices without a pronounced dialect (called general American speech and adopted by most media announcers). Public speeches without vocalized pauses ("um") are more esteemed.

The family of origin and root culture also teach children a dialect, how to have a conversation, and how long to pause when speaking. Each of these speech behaviors are, in turn, valued or devalued by others who learned different styles. Tannen (1990) suggested that two conversational styles are common: rapport and report. Each style has rules for how to be competent during a conversation. A *rapport conversational style* is cooperative, with one individual playing the supporting role while the other leads the conversation. In contrast, the *report conversational style* is a fun

Table 2.1

Perception's Impact on Communication

1. We judge ourselves more charitably than we judge others.
2. We attribute our behaviors to external circumstances and others' behaviors to internal character traits.
3. We favor negative impressions of others over positive ones.
4. We are influenced by what is most obvious.
5. We cling to first impressions.
6. We assume that others are like us.
7. We predict the reactions of others based on our perceptions of them.

Source: McCorkle and Reese (2010, pp. 58–59).

contest to see who can talk the longest and control the topic. Rapport style encourages nodding, agreement, telling stories on the same topic, and waiting for one's turn to speak (at which time the conversational leader and follower roles reverse). Report style requires assertive interruption to change the topic, speaking at length without pausing, and contesting who is in control. Individuals may make personality attributions about people with different conversational styles. Those who learned rapport feel report-talkers interrupt too much, are rude, probably are egotistical, and don't know how to have a conversation. Report-style speakers may view rapport speakers as unassertive, having little to say, and unprepared to have a conversation.

Similarly, linguistic scholars have discovered that regions within a language group may have a slower or faster sense of how long a pause should be before one person finishes speaking and the next begins—called *pause gap*. Some speakers may expect a four beat (or even longer) pause between one person's utterance and the next. These individuals allow a conversational pause to linger for a moment before speaking. Those with quicker pause gaps feel an uncomfortable silence, so they rush to fill it. Different pause gaps in working groups can chill the ability of those with longer pause gaps to contribute. Leaders of these groups must create space for everyone to have a chance to contribute.

Regional groups also develop perceptual stereotypes about dialect, accent, and correctness of grammar. Ask individuals from one part of the United States what people are like in other parts and stereotypical attributions often emerge: European Americans from New York frequently are stereotyped as pushy or aggressive (fast talkers with overlapping pause

Table 2.2

Barriers to Effective Listening

- Pretending to listen while focusing on other thoughts
- Interrupting (because my thoughts are more important)
- Remaining over-focused on personal needs
- Using selective attention and heeding only parts of a message (usually in readiness for the rebuttal)
- Letting emotions run free
- Acting on preconceptions about the person or the message
- Allowing external distractions (noise, other visual stimuli)
- Focusing on internal distractions (hunger)

gaps), southerners as a bit slow (languid pace of speech, distinct dialect, and longer pause gaps), and westerners are shallow and sometimes naive (smile a lot, use regional colloquialisms). The linguistic habits discussed here and many other aspects of communication are learned from family and regional culture.

Listening is the final area where notions of communication as an inborn talent linger. Listening is not the same as hearing. *Hearing* is the physical aspect of communication. For those who can hear, sounds enter the ears and are processed into data the brain can comprehend. *Listening* occurs in the mind as the sounds are organized and interpreted. Many variables inhibit a fair translation of someone's message (see Table 2.2). For example, normal conversation occurs at 125 to 150 words per minute. Most individuals can easily process up to 500 words per minute. The mind uses this free time on other things if energy is not invested in being present and engaging in the conversation. (Listening skills are discussed in detail in Chapter 4.)

The Fallibility of Message Transfer

When the modern communication discipline began to take shape in the 1950s, the idea of how communication worked was influenced by the emerging radio and television era. Human communication was seen as similar to radio broadcasts. Jeffrey has a *message* in mind. He *encodes* the mental idea into symbols and sends it out through the *channel* of spoken words. Madison, the recipient, *decodes* the message. If there isn't too much noise to impede Madison's hearing, the message should get across just fine. In this *mechanical model* developed by Shannon and Weaver in 1949, communication was one-way and existed in a sequential set of

---

Insights from the Field
The Value of Weekly Networking Meetings

Mark Rees, City Manager, Portland, Maine

The weekly staff meeting with my department heads is an example of one of my efforts to improve communication. We all sit around this circular table and I lead the conversation by talking about upcoming items—perhaps the City Council agenda and what needs to be done, issues of general interest to the department heads. Then I ask them all to go around and give a little update about their department and what they're working on. I encourage communication between the department heads because there's a lot of work that's being done that involves an interaction between the departments. Sometimes they don't know that what one department is doing can have an impact on another department.

---

encoded and decoded transmissions. Mechanical models are the origin of colloquialisms such as: We have a "communication breakdown" or "I need to take that comment back."

Modern scholars understand that communication does not work like a machine. Communication is not one-way. Instead, people continuously send and receive verbal and nonverbal messages.

Going from intended thought to encoded message is not a precise activity. Sometimes, communicators are unsure of their intentions—they talk and think about what to say at the same time. Sometimes thoughts are crystal clear, but the limitations of language blur efforts to communicate an idea precisely. The words and nonverbal communication may contradict each other, sending a *mixed message* to the recipient (who usually believes the nonverbal). Sometimes the surrounding context changes how a message is interpreted, a message recipient has a personal meaning (*connotation*) for words different than the originator, or a listener commits errors when decoding the message. In addition to the verbal level of message meaning, a nonverbal track also runs continuously. Intonation, facial expression, gestures, pauses, and body movement all carry culturally influenced information that is used to interpret messages. The communication process is fraught with opportunity for intended messages to go astray. While early communication models presented tidy boxes of meaning marching from one person to another in a unidirectional way, modern communication models look like wild scribbles—everything, going everywhere, all the time.

The notions that "I told you so you should understand" or that "you should understand what I mean" (even if I didn't articulate it very well) are formulas for misunderstanding. Communication is hard. Language is imprecise. Nonverbal communication can contradict the verbal. Meaning is elusive. Learning to verify the other person's understanding and to seek clarification are important communication skills.

Leadership and Communication

Leadership and facilitating change are two of the five core competencies in the *Senior Executive Service: Executive Core Qualifications* (U.S. OPM 2012). Leadership can mean many things, including moving others toward an organization's vision and goals, providing an inclusive workplace, facilitating cooperation through teamwork, or fostering the constructive resolution of conflict. However leadership is defined, it generally requires enhanced communication skills and perceptiveness about others' behavior. One of the variables that blocks the budding career advancement of technically competent employees is a lack of communication skill.

Management and leadership are not the same. "Manager" and "supervisor" are job titles that require accomplishment of specific tasks. Top executives in an agency and others with formal titles also need to be leaders. Leadership goes beyond making sure a task is accomplished. Leaders affect a unit or organization's culture, behavior, and expectations. Individuals, whether they carry formal authority or not, become leaders when others perceive value in following that person. Through their communication and behaviors, leaders induce others to listen, heed their words, and follow their examples. Managers who focus on rule infractions, hound staff to stay on task, or closet themselves in their offices may meet the technical requirements of a job, but rarely will be viewed as leaders.

Van Wart's (2003) review of leadership theory in the public sector differentiates between transformational and transactional leadership. *Transactional leadership* is task oriented and guided by specific goals. *Transformational leadership* focuses on overarching vision. Van Wart identified five general ways to define leaders in an administrative context (Table 2.3). How agencies define leadership usually influences how supervisors motivate employees and how an organization operates.

Table 2.3

Definitions of Leadership in the Public Sector

1. Leaders provide the results mandated for their unit in an efficient and legal manner.
2. Leaders develop subordinates who provide the results mandated for their unit in an efficient and legal manner.
3. Leaders align the organization with the changing environment and realign organization culture and mission as changes occur.
4. Leaders are servants to the people.
5. Leaders provide technical direction and performance with a public service orientation.

Source: Van Wart (2003).

The Dark Side of Positional Authority

Five leadership pitfalls await those who assume formal positions of authority without sufficient preparation or good communication skills: (1) self-focus, (2) counterproductive communication habits, (3) premature change, (4) anemic expectation management, and (5) skipping the apprentice stage.

Self-Focus

Being promoted to management or achieving the status of a directorship can be a heady experience. It is tempting to be seduced by the allure of personal power. Fletcher and Cooke (2012) of the Federal Executive Institute explain that good leaders are not self-absorbed. Effective leaders combine self-knowledge with understanding of others to select the right leadership strategy for each situation. Without reflection about self and others in the agency (subordinates, co-equals, and bosses), an individual's behaviors can be self-centered and out of step with the larger context. For example, those who acquire power abruptly rather than grow into it may think commanding employees to perform is enough—focusing on giving orders rather than understanding issues.

Supervisors who are self-focused miss opportunities to develop trust and loyalty among employees. *Followership* is the counterpart of leadership. When an organization has effective leaders, others want to follow and find the experience beneficial. When the experience is beneficial, those who follow engage in a vast array of positive organizational citizenship behaviors—they voluntarily act in ways that add value to the organization's goals rather than focusing primarily on personal goals. "Examples of [organizational citizenship behaviors] include helping coworkers with work-related problems, not complaining about trivial problems, behaving courteously to coworkers, and speaking approvingly about the organization to outsiders" (Zellars, Tepper, and Duffy 2002, p. 1068). Zellars et al. further determined that a quick way to derail organizational citizenship was through a supervisor's hostile or abusive language.

Counterproductive Communicative Habits

The farther up the ladder of authority one rises, the more time is spent meeting with and communicating with others (as opposed to working alone on specific tasks). Those selected for positions of authority because of their technical or scientific skills may face a steep learning curve in understanding employee motivation and replacing counterproductive communication habits with skills more suitable for leaders.

Some manager behaviors undercut leadership potential and employee morale. Even if a supervisor believes sarcasm or verbal abuse is an appropriate motivational strategy, research indicates abusive supervision results in higher tension and emotional exhaustion among employees (Breaux et al. 2008). Leaders set the tone for the entire workplace. The behavior a leader adopts makes a difference. Messages also are conveyed to employees when a leader observes a negative workplace behavior and does nothing about it. With regard to workplace bullying, Estes and Wang (2008) note "the words and actions of organizational leaders are watched carefully by employees and set an example for others" (p. 235). Leaders who tell sexist jokes, yell at subordinates, or exhibit passive-aggressiveness should not be surprised when their workforce becomes rife with similar behaviors that then escalate to actionable or illegal levels.

On the other end of the spectrum, supervisors may develop habits of inaction. For a variety of reasons, some supervisors do too little or are reluctant to enforce policies and regulations. When a few supervisors enforce policies and others do not, employees will perceive the agency as unfair. Lack of consistency also makes an organization vulnerable to grievances and litigation.

Other communication skill deficiencies can haunt those who are promoted. For example, a newly frocked manager may never have led a

Table 2.4

Leadership Responses to Worker Incivility

- Taking an honest look in the mirror at one's personal behaviors
- Weeding out incivility during the hiring process
- Teaching civility
- Listening carefully to what is happening in your organization
- Hammering incivility hard when it occurs
- Investing in post-departure interviews

meeting, interviewed a job applicant, intervened in an employee conflict, or established an interagency team. Prospective managers must seek out training and mentorship to broaden their competencies.

Premature Change

Novice leaders may think the first day on the job is the right time to order changes to workflow, unit goals, or agency traditions. In bureaucracies, the culture of an agency often persists in spite of changes in top executives. Leaders rely on followers to conform to the standards they set.

Insights from the Field
On Agency Culture

An Oregon Department of Transportation Human Resources Officer

Every agency that you look at has a different culture that is a result of history, leadership, choices they've made, experiences both good and bad. So every agency has some uniqueness to it. But a lot of the personnel issues have similarities. Probably 95 percent of your workforce will always have good intent and will always try to do the right thing. So, you spend all your time trying to deal with that other 5 percent. One of the things that struck me early in my career in HR occurred when I was talking to some staff people. I asked them, "So what are your thoughts or opinions?" Somebody raised their hand and said, "I'm really tired of paying for the sins of others." Which I thought was a very profound statement. So, my philosophy around this is we should trust employees until they give us a reason not to trust them. And we should never overreact because of one incident.

Insights from the Field
Best Practice in Change Management

Some Washington Department of Transportation state offices had the opportunity to move from twenty-eight different locations throughout the county into one building. The facilities and business services group put together a series of focus groups about what kinds of things to pay attention to in their new buildings. Part of that was setting behavior guidelines. How do you respect your neighbor when you work in a group work environment? For example, don't hang over their cubicle wall and talk to coworkers, and watch the level of your voice. Don't put a client on speaker and have a conversation with them. Employees from all units participated in the creation of the guidelines.

Yet organizational culture and loyalty among workers may trump a new executive's wishes.

New leaders with goals that vary from historic norms should consider change as a long campaign of persuasion rather than something that can be mandated or approached in a piecemeal fashion. Brehm and Gates (1997) comment:

> The structure of organizational cultures can have tremendous consequences for the prospects of attaining compliance. Conformity that stems from organizational culture can either induce or impede compliance with superiors. Bureaucratic supervisors will experience considerable difficulty in implementing policies that run counter to organizational norms. On the other hand, compliance will be very high in those cases where the organizational culture reinforces the supervisor's requests. (p. 55)

Good leaders rarely make unilateral decisions (except in an emergency). Leaders seek information before acting, listen, use consistent communication to build trust, and include others in change processes when feasible.

Anemic Expectation Management

Leaders set clear expectations for what subordinates are to do and trust workers to perform their jobs without micromanaging (applying the

Insights from the Field
Leaders Create the Work Environment

*Lt. Col. Orndorff, 2011 Commander Defense Contract
Management Agency, Boeing, Seattle*

My first day [at DCMA-Boeing as Commander], I took all my supervisors into a room and I laid it all on the table: here's what is important to me; here's what I feel strongly about; here's what I expect from you; here's the environment that I want to create. So, everybody in the room knows exactly where I'm coming from. I don't make them guess for the first six months. I intend to treat you this way. I intend you to take ownership of your responsibilities. Don't be late—I tell them right up front, your number one thing: don't be late on anything, don't miss a task, and we'll get along fine. So then when somebody brings a problem to me, I go back to that and I say, remember what I'm trying to create here is a positive, healthy work environment. So as you are working through your problem, I have the overall work environment in mind. I want to have one of the highest morale activities of my career. Because it's no fun slamming doors and having to be mad at people all the time. That's just not my style. I want to create an environment where people are laughing and working well together and I don't have to deal with them.

So I learned this trick from a general the first time I took command. He said: "Write down for yourself alone, what kind of environment you want to create." I did and thought about how to present my goals to my staff. Next, I sat down with my supervisors and told them what I wanted. I waited three weeks. Then I did a commander's call and I delivered the exact same information to the whole organization. Now everybody knows. Here's the game plan. It comes from my level down. So anybody out in my organization knows if I hear a door slamming and yelling, in any way shape or form, they know exactly what I'm going to do—they already know my expectation.

Q: What's your best tool for correcting workplace misbehavior?
A: Prevention. Be clear what my expectations are of workplace behavior on day one.

old adage: "trust, but verify"). A great deal of anxiety occurs whenever management positions turn over. What will the new manager want? Will things change? How should I behave? Leaders should be clear in setting expectations about work performance and behavior. Those who skirt laws, are uncivil, have poor communication skills, or seem unconcerned about productivity, inadvertently create low standards. If the leader does not set expectations, employees will guess, be guided by past habits, or conform to standards set by someone else in the organization—often the weakest employee.

Skipping the Apprentice Stage

All of the above issues can be exacerbated when individuals are promoted quickly based on their technical or scientific expertise. Those who wish to be leaders need to develop a wide repertoire of communication and technical skills. Advanced workshops, university classes, and internal training programs can provide information in many competency areas. Apprenticeships (formal or informal) create an arena for honing and testing skills. Chairing a committee is a precursor to running meetings for a department. Facilitating a taskforce can present an opportunity for learning about managing interagency partnerships.

Case: The New Boss

Helen was excited to start her new job at the state department of parks and recreation where she would be heading up a new program intended to encourage children to appreciate the outdoors. Only three months after completing her masters of public administration (MPA), Helen was eager to get started. She was concerned about whether the four employees who would be reporting to her would accept her authority. She knew the hiring committee had taken a chance in offering her the job and she had already made a list of changes she planned to announce at her first staff meeting.

As the staff gathered, Helen read from her notes: everyone should know that she intended to make some big changes, and quickly. She had drawn up a timeline, budget, goals, objectives, and key performance indicators that she distributed to the four employees. Helen was proud of the fact that she had utilized so many of the tools that she had learned in her MPA program. After handing out the timeline and goals, objectives and task lists, Helen quickly adjourned the meeting.

In an e-mail to her mentor at the university she wrote, "I wanted to make sure I was decisive and by the end of the meeting everyone knew

I was in charge." Later that week, Helen's boss called her into his office. She had expected to brief her boss on the great new changes she had instituted. As Mr. Gray set down at his desk he said, "We've got a problem. I have had several visits and e-mails from your team. Seems they're not too happy with how things are going." Helen was shocked. She thought she had gotten off to a great start.

Discussion Questions

1. What could Helen have done differently to get started on the right foot with her new team?
2. What steps can Helen take now to improve the situation with the team?

3

Resolving Disputes in the Workplace

Methods for Resolving Disputes

Public administrators play three primary roles with regard to conflict in the public sector: they are observers of conflict, they act as arbitrators or mediators in conflict resolution, or they are parties to the conflict (Lan 1997). Conflict can take place on the national or global stage (macro level). One example is the Kurds' struggle for equitable treatment by the governments of Turkey and Iraq. Conflict can also take place among individuals, on the micro level. For example, coworkers may disagree over the best methods to use on a project. Although many of the dynamics are similar in conflicts of any scale, we will focus on the micro level of public and nonprofit sector workers and their interactions with the public. Understanding how to confront, manage, and prevent conflict is a vital skill for public administrators. Effective conflict resolution can avoid expensive litigation, loss of good employees, or damage to productivity caused by soured work relationships.

Conflict management scholars explain that disputes at the individual level manifest from three different perspectives: power, rights, or interests. When acting from *power*, the one with the greatest political, economic, social, or physical leverage can force others to comply. The *rights* perspective applies rules or laws that grant privileges to individuals via seniority, union rules, or other policies. Those acting from *interests* attempt to find common ground and solutions that best meet everyone's needs.

The rights approach probably is the most familiar for public employees. Civil service rules or union contracts provide numerous rights and safeguards. Limitations arise when a grievance policy (the rights approach) is the sole option for employees who are in conflict. Lacking other avenues to solve a problem, employees may file grievances against each other. In these cases, small issues grow as people are placed into adversarial positions during a grievance procedure. Work relationships may suffer. In some cases, the substance of the conflict is not a grievable issue under the rule and the case is dismissed—yet the conflict and its negative impacts on the workplace endure. In other cases, a grievance hearing occurs without the employees speaking to one another. Someone wins; someone loses—and the original conflict may continue. Sometimes employees need the protection of grievance hearings. At other times, an employee who feels uncomfortable talking directly with a coworker just needs help.

More structural options are needed in public agencies and supervisors require skills to deal with employee conflicts in their infancy. Civil service rules and agency policies are not enough. Skilled supervisors can manage conflicts while they are small and before work relationships are irrevocably tainted. Agencies with options to formal grievances (supervisor coaching, problem-solving sessions, mediation, and so forth) create the opportunity to manage issues before they fester.

What Causes Workplace Conflict?

Conflict can occur when one person perceives someone else as interfering with accomplishment of an important goal (McCorkle and Reese 2010). Sometimes conflict is based on an accurate perception of interference from another person and sometimes the perception is false. As discussed in Chapter 2, human perception is imprecise and prone to error. Whether difficulties arise for good reasons or from misperceptions, conflict is the inevitable result.

All conflicts are not alike. Goal interference can arise from many sources. Conflict commonly originates in one of the following areas: power, relationships, substantive and task issues, emotion, information, structure, values, and style. The typology of conflict in the workplace is important as each type of conflict has unique elements and different management strategies apply.

Power

Power is paradoxical. Generally, people only think power is a problem when they feel powerless. Simply put, "power" is the ability to influence others. Power is problematic in many conflicts and deserves special attention.

Insights from the Field
Rules about Social Media

A Utah Human Resources Officer

We've had people Facebooking and complaining about their supervisor
or coworkers and others are commenting. They're stating on Facebook
that they work for our agency. We have disciplined them under the code
of ethics for being disrespectful to coworkers. So, we found a policy
that works to manage this behavior, but there's a lot of nuances to social
media. Can you befriend a client on social media? Our society is becoming so technology advanced, and it's become so intertwined that I think
there needs to be some clear guidance on what is and isn't appropriate
on social media.

Max Weber is familiar to students of public administration as the
theorist who first explained that the sources of government legitimacy
throughout history derived from the charisma of leaders, tradition, or the
rule of law (for a discussion of Weber and authority sources, see Stillman
2010). In the realm of general communication, the ability to influence
others was long viewed as coming from analogous interpersonal factors,
such as legitimate titles, control of resources, or possession of certain
characteristics. French and Raven (1959) delineated the five types of
traditional distributive power: reward (control over material resources),
coercion (control via fear of punishment), legitimate (control from position within a hierarchy), expert (control of knowledge or skills), and
referent (control from association with powerful others).

While traditional sources of power do exist, a more modern view
characterizes power as arising from connections among people. Power
can be located anywhere, not just in those at the top of the organizational
chart. When scholars began to abandon mechanical models of communication, they also reconceptualized ideas about power. Emerson (1962)
postulated that the power of one individual depended on how much
another individual needed what he or she possessed. In other words, if a
group does not respect your title or designated authority, you have little
influence (power) over them. Because of the connective nature of power,
modern perspectives recognize that we have power "with" people (as

an exchange) rather than "over" them. Any new supervisor who uses authority as a club soon discovers the many ways subordinates can sap an abusive leader's effectiveness.

New groups must negotiate how they will relate to each other to create a power structure. For example, resource power is not a constant; it is situational. A resource only becomes a source of power if the other person needs it. Respect, esteem, admiration, and technical expertise are all reasons individuals gift power to others. If one person is dependent on another for goal achievement, the dependence relationship creates power. If a work team needs to use a new piece of equipment and only one person can operate it, the knowledgeable one has potential power. The worker who knows everyone in the agency and can get information quickly has potential power through networking. Sometimes we allow others to influence us simply because we like the way a person looks or dresses (based on cultural ideals).

When new relationships or groups form, a natural process of creating the lines of connection among individuals occurs. People want to know if others have skills, characteristics, resources, and so forth that will help meet personal goals. Sometimes, a struggle for dominance erupts. When power struggles persist, they typically have negative outcomes: trust is reduced, miscommunication increases, and the ability to fulfill the agency's mission takes second place to the drive for personal domination.

One of the interesting dynamics anecdotally reported by conflict coaches is that if the individuals in a power struggle are asked who has more power, they will point at each other, each thinking the other has more power. Those who feel they are in a low power position may take steps to balance power. One way to balance power is to decrease dependence on the other person—literally leaving the situation, withdrawing support, disconnecting emotionally, or even striking out to demean the other person. When both individuals take steps to balance power, a move and counter-move spiral of negativity can occur. When someone yells or speaks aggressively, it may be because the individual feels powerless. In those cases, problem solving is a more effective response than mirroring the negative communication.

Power struggles also occur when a manager perceives subordinates as acting beyond their station—being "uppity" or intruding into the supervisor's work. While there are employees who will attempt to take power from their bosses and there are members of the public who do try to overwhelm a public sector worker, there also are people who have poor communication skills or are afraid to communicate with their superiors. Fear, discomfort, or shyness may be masked by anger, bluntness, or talking around the person one should be talking to—all behaviors that might look like power manipulations. Heifetz and Laurie (1997) put it this way: "The voices from below are usually not as articulate as one would wish. People speaking beyond their authority usually feel self-conscious and sometimes have to generate 'too much' passion to get themselves geared up for speaking out. Of course that often makes it harder for them to communicate effectively" (p. 129). Interest and concern sometimes are better responses to anger than zero tolerance policies or overreactions. "Rather than view these expressions as inherently hostile acts and/or personal affronts or challenges to authority, management could be taught to recognize that employee anger helps them identify workplace conditions requiring significant and/or immediate attention" (Geddes and Stickney 2010, p. 224). Coaching an angry employee toward more productive communication behaviors is recommended.

Public sector employees may need to deny citizen requests for services or be unable to help due to regulatory constraints. Denial of services may squash personal goals and bring up feelings of powerlessness. Ury (2007), in *The Power of a Positive No*, explains that saying "no" is uncomfortable, so people may avoid it by attacking or blaming another person or expressing resentment. Ury recommends avoiding the accusatory "you" when denying a request. Instead of saying "You should have done this earlier, before the deadline," one can say: "The deadline was yesterday; here is the information about the appeal process after the deadline." Ury recommends removing the word "no" from one's vocabulary because it evokes an automatic defensive reaction in listeners. Instead of vocalizing the word "no," move on to what you would have said next. The word "no" becomes invisible even though the rest of the message remains the same.

Many strategies exist for manipulating power in appropriate and beneficial ways. The strategy chosen depends on the power dynamic between individuals. In general, conflict management occurs best when neither party feels powerless. Table 3.1 presents several ways to manage power.

Another contributor to relationship and power conflict is the human tendency to commit attribution errors. We unconsciously filter external data that arrives through our senses to match preconceived ideas (see Chapter 2). We also fit bits and pieces of disparate information into stories that may or may not match reality. We attribute meaning to others' actions

Table 3.1

Strategies to Manage Power

- Ask genuinely curious questions (Chapter 4)
- Metacommunicate about the pattern of communication
- Show respect
- Say "No" gracefully
- Apply power to advance group goals more than to advance personal goals
- Use power more to reward than to punish or intimidate
- Empower others by working on solutions together
- Share your perception that there is a power struggle going on
- Avoid responding to the other person's early offers and self-interested frames
- Start with discussion of the process, how decisions will be made, or rules for civility during the session
- Take a break or postpone
- Comment on how you are interdependent and need each other to accomplish a goal
- Make a stronger connection to something the other values

Every tactic is not appropriate in every situation. Select the appropriate tactic based on your analysis of the situation and the individuals involved.

regardless of their intentions. While there is some debate as to the cognitive processes involved in the nuances of attribution (see Funder 2001), individuals do judge the behaviors and motives of others. An *internal attribution* interprets another individual's behavior as deriving from his or her personality. For example, someone making an internal attribution about an angry individual would see the anger as a personality defect in the other person. In the same situation, if we attribute the anger to be due to transient situational factors, such as receiving an adverse decision, it is an *external attribution*. Labeling a person's behavior as internal may lead to more negative response strategies than perceiving a behavior as situational, or external. We tend to see our own behaviors as driven by situations and others' by their personalities.

Relationships

Conflict can arise when individuals do not have the same perception of what their relationship is or should be. What does it mean to be a boss and a subordinate? Must coworkers attend department social events after work hours? Should coworkers share personal information with each other? Is a public sector employee working "for" a specific member of the public?

Managing relationship conflict requires discussion of boundaries or work roles and responsibilities. These discussions can be difficult and special attention should be paid to avoiding embarrassment. When behavior is perceived as intending to humiliate or demean, emotion-based conflict can result. When responding to relationship conflict, it is particularly important to allow the other individual to escape with his or her self-image intact—to avoid intentional or unintentional humiliation. Instead of confronting a subordinate for "sticking his nose into everybody else's job," the discussion can be framed as "I think there may be some confusion about each person's job responsibilities. Let's review what is and what is not each person's job."

Substantive and Task Issues

Task or substantive conflicts are about resources, scheduling, job parameters, and more tangible items. These conflicts can have positive results if they are managed well. Conflict can energize the team, clarify resource utilization, or bring creativity to a situation. However, an environment of high task conflict has been correlated with the emergence of bullying (Ayoko, Callan, and Hartel 2003).

Information

When disagreement arises about which data to use or what data is accurate, an information conflict exists. This type of conflict may also occur when people unknowingly apply disparate data sets, use terminology differently, or withhold important information. In the public sector, partisan differences may lead to reliance on separate studies or interpretations of data. For example, a citizen may quote a favorite talk radio commentator as if that individual's opinions are proven fact. Misunderstanding or confusion can abound.

In addition, access to confidential information can give organizational members a sense of power over others. Information asymmetry occurs when one person has access to information another does not.

If an information conflict emerges, it is important to clarify which data each participant is using and engage in early discussion of the criteria by which data should be selected. While keeping data secret is a common competitive business practice, there are few reasons to withhold data from the public, and often there is a legal obligation to disclose. If information conflicts are looming, it is important to put data on the table.

Skill Development
Problem Solving Around Data

If an information-based conflict exists, the beginning steps of the problem-solving process may be helpful.

1. Clarify the task
   a. Frame the issue productively
   b. Define key terms
   c. Set a timeline (end date for a decision)
   d. Decide how to decide the outcome (majority vote, designated leaders decided, consensus, accept opinion of agreed-upon consultant or arbiter)
   e. Discuss the consequences if no agreement is reached
2. Set criteria for an acceptable solution
   a. Technical parameters (policy)
   b. Social components (people and relationships)
3. Put data on the table about the issue
   a. What already is known about the problem?
   b. What is not known that needs to be discovered?
   c. What skills or "helps" need to be developed?
4. Suggest solutions
5. Evaluate solutions to criteria and culture
6. Select and implement the plan

Methods for resolving information conflicts are presented in the box on "Skill Development: Problem Solving around Data."

Emotion

Emotion and hurt feelings are a common cause of conflict and may overlay other types, which creates a doubling effect. When emotion is paired with substantive, relationship, or other types of conflict, it is necessary to overcome the emotional barriers before problem solving can occur. When people are emotional, feel hurt, or harbor a grudge, they do not listen and may misinterpret even well-intended messages. Whether the emotional conflict is caused by an intended action or through a misinterpretation, once the emotional barrier exists it requires work to surpass the resulting negativity.

Table 3.2

Tactics to Defuse Emotions

- Emotional paraphrase (Chapter 4)
- Avoid escalating trigger words or behaviors
- Use "I" when expression one's ideas and avoid the accusatory "You" ("I need to take a break when the discussion gets too loud" rather than "You need to not be so angry")
- Describe behaviors rather than evaluate, judge, or make personality attributions
- Talk about common goals when the discussion gets heated to remind everyone of what you share in common
- Ask the other person how he/she feels about the discussion
- Help the other person save face

Verbal intonations, sarcasm, thoughtless or hurtful comments are common causes of emotional conflict. An offhand critical comment from a manager can be interpreted by an employee as an insult. A boss who intends good-natured banter about a worker's mismatched socks may be perceived as maliciously embarrassing that employee. We frequently are more charitable toward ourselves than others—thinking that our comments don't mean anything in particular; but others' comments are fraught with significance.

Gibb (1961) contrasted the types of communication behaviors that cause conflict with those that help prevent conflict. Defense-provoking behaviors include sarcasm, passive aggressiveness, superiority, claiming rightness, and other egocentric forms of speech. Verbal aggression and sarcasm, particularly from supervisors, usually are perceived as attacks (Calabrese 2000). Supervisors should eschew evaluative sarcasm and instead coach employees. For example, an employee who habitually uses sarcasm can be coached to use more team-oriented comments while at work. Escalation and emotional reactions can be triggered when words or tone of voice are perceived as aggressive, the other person is seen as acting unfairly, the social or interpersonal bond between people begins to weaken, and the large problem being addressed becomes more difficult to solve (Friedman and Currall 2003).

Structure

Types of structural conflicts include how projects are organized, how physical space is utilized, and how decisions are made. Structure can also

Table 3.3

Skills to Respond to Structural Conflict

- Determine if specific processes are required by rule or if they can be designed by the agency
- Discuss criteria for the best arrangement
- Use a problem-solving process (see the Skill Development box)

relate to the rules that govern collaborative arrangements in public administration. Structural conflicts can be associated with power struggles. For example: if two members of a task force argue about the sequence of the steps that will be taken to implement a project, the apparent conflict is structural (how to do a task), but the underlying conflict may be a struggle for who is in control of the group.

Public information sessions may cause conflict if the public was expecting an opportunity to give input about a decision that has already been made. Structural conflicts can emerge around how to sequence a task or the timeline for a decision. Table 3.3 outlines methods for managing structural conflict.

Values

Value conflicts among employees may arise when individuals have differing lifestyles, religions, or political affiliations. Personal value conflicts are manageable if an agency has a mechanism to supplement state and federal antidiscrimination laws. Workplace values of teamwork and equitability should supersede the expression of personal values at work. It is not necessary for everyone to have the same values, but individual value expressions that interfere with work should not be permitted. If policies exist to govern the expression of personal values at work and if these policies are applied uniformly across all employees, value conflicts can be moderated in the workplace with relative ease (see Table 3.4).

More problematic conflicts emerge when a program or the agency mission involves competing value structures. Values can be expressed in ideological constructs that individuals use to evaluate behaviors. For example, the construct for agency accountability can be quite different depending on whether an individual values social welfare or individual autonomy. For example, those who value the betterment of social welfare for everyone may want to invest resources in increasing the speed of responding to service requests and try to help more people. Those

---

Table 3.4

Options for Managing Workplace Value Conflict

- Leverage workplace value or respect policies to highlight positive workplace behaviors
- Use outside facilitators to create a statement of values or workplace respectful behaviors
- Add worker collegiality measures to the evaluation process
- Review workplace respect policies and expectations with new employees and during scheduled employee evaluation meetings
- Provide training on proactive communication skills for a unit exhibiting value conflict

---

valuing individual autonomy might believe people could figure out their own problems if government didn't race to the rescue and prefer to have fewer employees working at service requests.

When value structures collide, intractable or thorny conflicts may emerge. If fiscal cutbacks are unavoidable, all employees may agree that the agency's mission has to be maintained but disagree about which programs are most essential. Even though everyone may agree that national security is important, widespread disagreements arise on how to achieve it. Most agencies will experience some types of value conflict, either internally or externally.

The challenge in managing value conflict exists in creating an environment where opinions can be expressed without rancor, where disagreements are civil, and where consensus procedures are used (when possible). If value conflict situations are allowed to fester, work units become emotionally savaged and distrust among public stakeholders may increase. In acknowledgment of the difficulty of these processes, some agencies have developed guidelines for creative and collaborative decision processes. For example, the Technical Service Center of the U.S. Geological Survey released a technical memorandum, *Resolving Disputes over Science in Natural Resource Agency Decisionmaking* (Ruell, Burkardt, and Clark 2010). (See Chapter 10 for some processes used during public comment periods that are useful for value conflicts.)

Style

Individuals have firm preferences on how to behave and communicate. A "style" is a preferred way of acting. When styles clash, workers may

Table 3.5

Tactics for Ameliorating Style Conflicts

- Observe that a difference might just be from individual styles
- State your style and your observation of the other person's style
- Determine if it doesn't really make much difference how the task is accomplished
- Comment that you're glad you've figured out the style difference and you hope now both of you won't be bothered by something that doesn't really matter:

> Hi, Jacob. I just noticed something kind of funny that I wanted to tell you about. Every morning I come in and put the stapler and the hole punch up on the counter thinking it will be easier for everybody to find. I just figured this out by seeing you come in and put the stapler and hole punch back on the desk. I don't know if you noticed but we've been doing that about three times a day. It probably really doesn't matter where the stapler is and I'm not going to move it anymore up on to the counter. I thought I'd share my observation of our style differences with you. If you notice any other style things, let's talk about them before we annoy each other moving stuff around. What do you think?

engage in conflict over which way is best. These episodes manifest as gnawing feelings that another person speaks or acts inappropriately. Sometimes style conflicts are enacted by telling the other person he or she is wrong—"You're not folding the papers correctly"; "You're not working fast enough"; "You're too disorganized when you run a meeting." Typically, evaluating someone's style as "wrong" is not helpful.

The first step in managing style conflicts is to differentiate between style clashes that "feel" wrong but make no difference to work productivity and dissent over how to complete tasks that have safety, rule, or substantive impacts. Sometimes, there is one safe or legal way to accomplish a task. In these cases, substance should trump style. In many cases, however, style is the heart of conflict over whose way of acting is correct when there are many potential "right" answers.

Recognizing common areas where preferences clash is the beginning of style conflict management. Next, one must express the style difference to the other person in a way that does not create defensiveness (see Table 3.5).

Some individuals escalate and some fractionate when faced with new problems. The "escalator" style characterizes an individual who becomes excited and speaks more loudly or forcefully while declaiming (usually negatively) about the issue. Fractionators immediately become calm and move to problem solving. When extremes in each style meet, the escalator attributes the fractionator's behavior to a lack of involvement or caring. The fractionator sees the escalator's behavior as uncontrolled and foolish. Fractionators who are aware of the style difference can refrain from defensive-provoking comments such as, "If you weren't so emotional, we could work this out." Fractionators also can work to show involvement by speaking a bit louder than usual when paraphrasing while the escalator travels through the initial wave of expression. Then, both parties are more ready to move to problem solving.

People also may have distinct conflict management styles. Because of social consequences, most managers and many citizens learn to adapt, using the appropriate style for the occasion and people involved. In general, three styles predominate among European-Americans: competition, mutual gains, and avoidance (see Chapter 8).

Those who prefer avoidance pretend a conflict does not exist or use passive-aggressive tactics to express the conflict. Avoidance may be appropriate when the issue is not important, time is precious, or the interaction with the person is a one-time, fleeting event.

A competition style (also called distributive) views difference as a win-lose contest for emotional or substantive dominance. Tactics are chosen to maximize self-interested goal attainment. When resources are scarce, ethical competition is appropriate.

Mutual gains conflict management (also called integrative, collaborative, cooperative, or win-win) exhibits a preference for searching for solutions that benefit all parties. (For an in-depth discussion of each conflict management style and its related tactics, see McCorkle and Reese 2010.)

Case: Flextime

This case study has two parts. Read Part A and respond to the question, then proceed to Part B before reading the remainder of the case.

Part A

To: All Department Heads
From: Human Resources, City of Edgetown
Date: January 1, 2014

Pursuant to Edgetown ordinance number 525-14, all departments will institute a flextime policy to allow employees to meet their work and life obligations. The policy has the following conditions for employees to meet their 40-hour workweek.

1. Employees may complete the 40-hour workweek using any combination of time between 6 AM and 6 PM Monday through Friday.
2. No more than 40 hours can be worked in any single week.
3. Computation of sick leave, vacation, and overtime is the same for all employees, including those using flextime.
4. Flextime schedules will be evaluated after a three-month implementation period.
5. Flextime scheduling is at the discretion of the department. Decisions about whether staffing coverage is adequate to meet the operating requirements are made at the department level.

To: Employees of the City Clerk's Office, Edgetown
From: W. Trottier, Department Head, City Clerk's Office
Date: January 1, 2014

The city has implemented the new flextime policy that I'm sure you've all heard about already. Beginning Monday, anyone wishing to work a flexible schedule should contact me to sign up. Thanks!

Discussion Question

1. What could possibly go wrong with this scenario? Is there a better way to implement this policy?

Part B

To: Wendy Trottier
From: Bob Smith
Date: January 1, 2014

Hi Wendy, I'd like to sign up for flextime so that I can pick up Bobby Junior at the bus stop at 3:30. I'll come in at six o'clock and leave at three o'clock with an hour for lunch.

To: Wendy T.
From: Dawn Raines
Date: January 10, 2014

Wendy, I need to do the flexible scheduling so that I can be home with the kids. My husband's mom can't take them after school anymore and with no raises these past years we can't afford a babysitter!

To: Wendy
From: John Freeman
Date: Jan. 12, 2014

I'm training for the Boston Marathon and need to leave at 3:30 over the next months. I'll come in early to get my eight hours in. Thanks!

To: John Freeman
From: Wendy Trottier
Date: Jan. 12, 2014

John, we need coverage at the front desk in the late afternoon and Bob and Gwen are already leaving early to deal with their kids.

To: Wendy
From: John Freeman
Date: Jan. 15, 2014

I don't think it's fair that parents are hogging up all the flextime slots! You are discriminating against those of us who don't have kids! Just because I'm not babysitting my priorities aren't valued! I'll be talking to human resources about this later!

To: Wendy Trottier
From: Angela Smart
Date: Jan. 15, 2014

Hi Wendy, I have great news: I got a spot in the MPA class I wanted to help me prepare our upcoming performance management proposal. That flextime policy came out just in time! I'll need to leave by four o'clock on Thursdays to get to campus on time. Thanks for encouraging me to get started on my MPA.

Discussion Question

1. What should Wendy do to deal with the multiple requests for flextime scheduling? Is e-mail the best way to manage this?

4

Mega-Skills for Public Employees

While there is a cornucopia of skills that can be acquired, this chapter focuses on three mega-skills for public managers: listening, asking questions, and analyzing conflicts. The chapter ends with one arena in which the mega-skills are applied—interviewing.

Listening

> *The average person suffers from three delusions: (1) that he is a good driver, (2) that he has a good sense of humor, and (3) that he is a good listener.*
> —Former University of Southern California President, Steven B. Sample

One of the skills most needed by supervisors and public employees is the ability to listen. Listening allows a leader to learn about how work is most efficiently accomplished, to discover employee strengths and weaknesses, and to discern the hopes and fears of the public. The person who either talks too much or attends too little has less chance to discover what is really going on in a situation. Without understanding the underlying drivers of a situation, problem-solving efforts become inefficient exercises in futility.

Listening is a civil behavior. When individuals disagree, there is a predisposition to stop listening—as if the act of attending to opposing views somehow equates with agreement. Listening is related to understanding others; it is not the same as agreement. Those exercising superficial listening sometimes fall into the semihumorous (to observers) condition of arguing even though they are in perfect harmony—sometimes called pseudo-conflict or faux agreement (Bartholome 2003). The arguers assume there is disagreement when none exists.

For public employees, listening is essential. If an employee misunderstands a service need, time and money can be wasted. Sometimes real

---

Skill Development
Collaborative Listening

Use When: There is a need to understand the other's viewpoint
General Rule: Collaboration cannot be achieved without each person
having an opportunity to speak and be understood

Step 1. Ask an **open-ended question**
Step 2. To indicate your understanding of the general issue, **reframe** or **summarize**
Step 3. Continue to let the other person speak to elaborate on his/her idea
Step 4. Ask a follow-up, non-defense provoking question to probe the other person's intention or idea details
Step 5. Shift the conversation to your thoughts by linking your idea to the other person's ideas
Step 6. (If necessary) Ask the other person to give you the same courtesy you gave to him/her so you can express your thoughts.

---

harm results. When a citizen feels a public employee has not or will not listen, frustration or anger may result. When intractable problems exist, listening and informing a citizen of policies or appeal processes may be all there is to offer.

Two fundamental listening skills should be in every public manager's toolbox: collaborative listening and emotional paraphrasing. Collaborative listening creates space for others to speak and provides an opportunity to discover underlying needs (i.e., interests). Some individuals are hesitant to state their genuine interests until they are sure someone really will listen. The "Collaborative Listening" skill development box (see above) describes the steps in collaborative listening. Ironically, the art of collaborative listening begins by asking a question. The question, however, must be open-ended and crafted to draw general information from the other person. "What is the concern?" or "What is going on in the situation?" and similarly open questions allow the responder to volunteer information. Starting the process with specific probes or incautiously phrased questions may divert the problem-solving process onto unproductive paths. Asking "Why do you want that service?" or "What's wrong with the policy?" may elicit defensiveness. In fact, any question

Skill Development
Emotional Paraphrasing: The Procedure

- Notice that the other person is extremely intense or emotional
- Listen, to determine the underlying tone
- Overlap the person's emotional speech with an emotional paraphrase of up to eight words, using the formula below (i.e., talk at the same time)
- Stop talking and listen
- Do not change the topic: ask questions, summarize, content paraphrase, or agree/disagree (these techniques may be used later but not in concert with emotional paraphrasing)
- Use one to three emotional paraphrases maximum, then move to an open-ended question

The Formula

Introduction	+	State of Mind Reflection
You seem/sound		. . . really bothered, angry, sad
		. . . frustrated, scared, concerned
That must have been		. . . difficult, awkward, frustrating

that begins with "Why?" seems to ask for a defensive or argumentative response. In general collaborative listeners ask questions and find interests before moving toward problem solving.

When someone is overly emotional or intense, the emotional paraphrase technique may be prudent. This helps a person move through the intensely emotional experience more quickly. It is in the problem solver's best interest to help an emotional speaker because research indicates intense emotions short-circuit the reasoning processes; that is, individuals who are angry, crying, or venting literally are not thinking clearly. Trying to move someone in an emotional state to problem solving too soon wastes time and effort. Instead, people on the receiving end of highly emotional speech can use skills like emotional paraphrasing or postponement to diffuse the situation.

The purpose of emotional paraphrasing is to make a connection with the other person without agreeing or disagreeing with the content of what they're saying. The procedure is described in the skill development box ("Emotional Paraphrasing: The Procedure" above). Once the distraught individual notices that someone will listen, he or she usually will moderate the verbal intensity and be more ready to move to problem solving.

If the situation is too intense or emotional paraphrasing is not effective, postponement might be preferable. This strategy works best when three criteria are met. First, the reason for postponement is expressed in personal terms rather than by blaming the other person: "I have a hard time listening when the conversation gets too loud. Let's meet again later when we've had some time to think about it." Second, the postponement is to a definite time rather than a general put-off: "Let's pick up this conversation this afternoon at 3:00 if that works for you." Finally, the postponement should give both parties positive homework to preempt brooding about the situation: "Before we meet again, let's both try to think of an outcome that might work for both of us." Research indicates some individuals will experience high stress and continue to fret about a situation if given too much time or not diverted into a more future-focused frame (Cloven and Roloff 1991).

Asking Questions

Asking questions is the second mega-skill for conflict managers. Early in an encounter, open-ended questions often are the best technique. Later in the exchange, genuinely curious and probing questions can be applied strategically.

Open-ended questions leave others room to respond. When someone asks: "What is the difficulty?" it allows choice in how to answer. In contrast, closed-ended or detail-oriented questions require specific answers. A supervisor whose first question is "How can the software be fixed?" presumes the problem is the software. Sometimes, subordinates may be hesitant to volunteer a different opinion—that the hardware is the problem. Asking specific questions too soon can cause misunderstandings and be inefficient.

When conversing with subordinates or less powerful individuals, the first specific topic mentioned by the supervisor sets the frame for the conversation. Others may comply with what they perceive as the supervisor's wishes. It is easy to waste time problem solving around the wrong issue when we neglect to invest a few moments to ensure that everyone is thinking about the same problem in the same way.

Table 4.1

Open-Ended Questions

Pre-plan several open-ended questions to start a conversation. For example:

- "What is it about _____ that concerns you?"
- "What are you trying to accomplish with this proposal?"
- "What are your thoughts about _____?"
- "Could you tell me more about what has been going on?"

When it is important to understand the other's perspective, underlying issues, or real needs, a safe forum must be created to elicit conversation. Open-ended questions fish for information without provoking defensiveness. When a difficult conversation is anticipated, it is useful to pre-plan several open-ended questions before the meeting.

Genuinely curious questions are a way to discover the other's intentions and avoid overreacting. When a comment spurs a defensive impulse, hold back from an argumentative retort and ask a question about the other's intention. For example, "When you say the project is stupid, what are you thinking about?" "You say you think I intentionally tried to embarrass you. I'm really stumped by that, can you tell me more?" "You say you have to have more independence. I'm curious, what were you thinking when you used the word 'independence'"? Genuinely curious questions elicit information without jumping to defensive conclusions.

Genuinely curious questions are paradoxical in several ways. First, when an individual feels attacked, asking for more information seems counterintuitive. The genuinely curious question, however, gives the other person a chance to clarify (I can still take offense later if my worst fears about the situation are true). Some of the individuals we work with will have less developed communication skills or may use provocative styles to get attention. The genuinely curious question allows less skilled communicators a second chance while providing more accurate information about that person's intentions. The initial reaction to someone's comments may be tainted by personal biases, experiences, and an assortment of attribution errors. The genuinely curious question helps prevent mistakes and galloping to the wrong conclusions.

Probing questions are useful later in a conversation after an initial picture emerges about the issue and the other person's needs. Probing questions search for detail:

- "What are your three best ideas on what might be done?"
- "If ___ happened, how would that affect you?"
- "When did you get the letter denying your application?"
- "How did this work for you in the past?"

Insights from the Field
Best Practices in Moderating Conflict

A combination of the research literature and interviews with state agency leaders provides a clear picture of how to moderate conflict. Agencies and departments with the best track records in managing employee conflicts do not try to write a policy to cover every imaginable employee infraction and then discipline anyone who steps out of bounds. As one official from the Utah Department of Human Resources explained, "We don't want to get into the habit of making a policy for every type of misconduct because then you lead people to believe that if it's not in policy, you can't discipline. And we don't want to go there because we can't ever cover every situation." Instead, these successful units write broad codes of conduct that describe respectful and productivity-based guidelines to supplement existing state and agency policies. Then they foster a culture that expects respectful communication and cooperation among all employees—from top to bottom of the organizational chart. These agencies train front line supervisors and managers to embrace the culture of respect and foster it in others. They also task upper management and human resources to keep standards and disciplinary actions consistent throughout agencies that often are widely dispersed, for example, a person in one part of the state who commits a minor violation cannot be fired for the first offense if employees in other parts of the state are coached and given a performance improvement plan about future behavior. Employees who slip into disrespectful or unproductive behaviors are coached toward better behavior instead of immediately moving into progressive disciplinary actions. For example, in Nevada they might give an employee a letter of instruction that sets out the standards and expectations so there is no ambiguity about behaviors. It is more about creating a better future workplace than catching infractions. Human resource officers help supervisors with coaching strategies and advise on when to move issues into progressive disciplinary actions. In sum, agency heads may be critical in sparking a positive culture, but front line supervisors guide the expectations for and performance of employees on a day-to-day basis.

The advice mentioned earlier also applies here: In communication, words matter; during interpersonal conflict, a heightened sensitivity to the ambiguous and slippery nature of language is essential.

Conflict Analysis

The ability to analyze a conflict prior to selecting a response is the third mega-skill for conflict managers. The following discussion focuses on two analytical tools: discovering the basic cause and mapping. Any combination of these tools can reveal important aspects of a situation and help the conflict manager decide what to do.

Discovering the Basic Cause

As discussed in Chapter 3, there are several clusters where conflict commonly arises: relationship, power, substantive, emotion, information, structure, value, and style. Identifying the most likely basic cause helps the conflict manager create an initial theory about the conflict and plan a management strategy.

All conflict management strategies require transformation of some element of a conflict. Various conflicts, however, may require different transformational strategies. Each conflict type has a different natural starting point. Knowing where to begin can decrease frustration and increase the probability of managing the conflict.

If a relationship or power is at the heart of the issue, begin by discussing roles, responsibilities, or boundaries. If a conflict is about substantive issues (budget, staffing, division of resources) more traditional bargaining is used. Discussions of how resources match agency goals can help in prioritizing substantive needs.

Emotional conflicts may arise when individuals become frustrated while working on another type of conflict (such as a difficult budget meeting) or when someone feels offended. When emotional conflicts are piled on top of another type of conflict, it is helpful to work on the emotional conflict first, then return to the main conflict. Individuals who feel offended or excluded are less likely to work in good faith during problem solving. If emotion (such as hurt feelings) is the primary cause of a conflict, it may be expressed as if it were a substantive conflict, that is, we may be fighting over paperclips (the apparent issue), but the real issue is "I don't feel you treat me with respect" (the emotional cause). In these cases, no amount of positive negotiation about paperclips will help the problem. When "respect" is discussed and individuals agree on workplace respect behaviors (the emotional issue), the substantive issue (paperclips) may disappear.

Structural conflicts are about how to organize a task or how to arrange items in a geographic space. It is useful to start transforming these conflicts by reviewing the constraints in the situation. Are there rules or regulations that govern how a process will unfold? Are there reasons other than personal style preference for organizing a project in a particular way? Talking about rules, procedures, customs, personal styles, and constraints is helpful during structural conflicts.

Value conflicts can be thorny, particularly in a political environment that allows polarization. In some cases, agency values in the workplace will trump personal values—employees are expected to follow the law, be respectful to coworkers and the public, and be professional. In other cases, decisions about how to implement policy goals invoke value differences. A mutual gains approach to value conflict allows individuals to express their values (if appropriate), seeks transcending values where the parties agree, and in many cases, notes that all parties will never fully agree on what is the best outcome. Ranchers, developers, environmentalists, dirt bike riders, hikers, bird watchers, and hunters may never agree on the best use for federally owned lands. We can, however, use processes that foster civil discussion among those who disagree while searching for the best outcome, which takes into account all of the constraints and competing interests. (See Chapter 10 for more details on these processes.)

If information confusion is the basic cause, it makes sense to start by talking about data: Who has what data? Do we have the same data? What criteria should we use to choose the data?

Mapping Interests

As stated earlier, an interest is an underlying need (versus a position, which demands a particular solution). Positions are the tip of an iceberg held up by a deep substructure of needs that lurk unexpressed beneath the waterline and out of view. When problem solving occurs at the position level, the underlying needs might be missed. These needs, still unmet, will reappear cloaked in a new positional costume. For example, an employee may approach his supervisor to ask for a new chair (the position). A busy supervisor may say "OK, order a chair." The employee returns the next week and asks for a new keyboard and the following week a new moni-

Figure 4.1   **Mapping the Conflict**

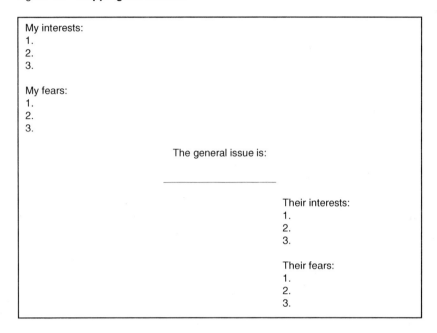

My interests:
1.
2.
3.

My fears:
1.
2.
3.

The general issue is:

_____

Their interests:
1.
2.
3.

Their fears:
1.
2.
3.

tor. Without taking the time to ask questions to find what lies below these positional demands, the manager may miss the underlying interest. Managers may feel as if they have "solved" several problems, but really they only reacted to positions that were masking the real issue. Acting based on positions is inefficient and may waste time and precious resources.

Mapping is a visual analytical tool created to discover interests. As Figure 4.1 illustrates, a general issue is written in the middle of a worksheet. The top portion of the page records the conflict from the mapper's perspective: What are my needs or interests in this issue? What are my fears if the issue is not resolved well? The bottom portion is a good faith estimation of the other person's perspective: What are his or her needs or interests in the situation? What are his or her fears if the issue isn't resolved well? Mapping provides information on several levels. First, when several interests are identified, it helps prevent the assumption that we know what the other individual's real interest is and prompts the asking of more questions before jumping to problem solving. Second, common needs or fears may emerge and expand the conflict manager's view of the situation.

Those using mapping as a diagnostic tool must be careful to avoid negative attribution when estimating the other's needs and fears. Be thoughtful when listing to the other person's probable needs and fears rather than hypercritical. Listing items such as: "He needs to be a jerk" or "She needs to make me look bad" rarely are helpful.

Assessing Cost-Effectiveness of Dispute Resolution

As with any work effort, a cost-benefit analysis of conflict management intervention is useful. Some sources claim supervisors spend about 20 percent of their time managing employee differences as a routine part of their job (Masters and Albright 2002). The percentage of management effort spent increases as conflicts mature or become intractable. In general, effort by management is worthwhile if the conflict behaviors affect unit goal achievement or taint employee relationships in ways that affect the work effort (i.e., the cost of management inaction is high). However, if supervisors intervene in every disagreement every day, employees will not learn to manage their own difficulties. Likewise, when a conflict exceeds a supervisor's training or abilities, it may be cost-effective to spend the time (and money) for an external specialist to facilitate or mediate employee conflict.

Whatever strategies are selected, upper management should perceive that the timing is right for the effort to have impact (i.e., cost-effective in time or fees), employees must believe the intervention is fair, and follow-up must provide accountability. Examples of some of the tools used to manage employee conflict are detailed in Table 4.2.

Interviews

Interviews occur for many reasons. Conducting a good interview is a leadership activity. Poorly constructed interviews can lead to inefficiency in task or service performance, poor employee coaching, or hiring new employees who are dispositionally or technically unfit for the job. Effective interviews are a combination of planning and perspicuity in interpreting the interviewee's responses.

Preparing for the Interview

Interviews can be more productive by preparing for three phases: before the interview, during the interview, and after the interview. Interviews

Table 4.2

Conflict Management Tools in Organizations

- Train employees to settle their differences without outside help
- Establish policies and procedures about appropriate workplace behavior and employee responsibilities to manage conflict
- Encourage informal discussion with supervisors when conflicts occur
- Establish genuine open door policies by supervisors to give employees access
- Distribute employee satisfaction surveys to discover pockets of discontent
- Offer a confidential hot line
- Use neutral facilitators to guide groups in conflict
- Offer mediation or arbitration options
- Coach employees and supervisors to improve communication
- Include informational or formal problem solving meeting as part of grievance procedures
- Create an ombudsperson position

Source: Adapted in part from Olson-Buchanan and Boswell (2009).

can be very formal (hiring) or informal (structured conversation). Any meeting with another person to seek information is an interview— even if we call it an informal meeting over coffee. The following discusses interviewing from each side of the table: the interviewee and the interviewer.

Prior to an interview, the most important determinant is deciding one's purpose. What information acquisition (or sometimes information conveyance) is the primary goal? Review the other individual's background, current position, and working preference. With background information in hand, set an appointment. To arrange an interview, appeal to the other person's interests, for example, "I'd like to talk with you about your experiences with contract negotiations, since I heard that your city has done very well in that area." After the interview time and place is secured, prepare an interview question list. Even informal information-gathering sessions will benefit from well-prepared questions. In formal hiring interviews, the questions asked dramatically affect the quality of the information gained. Soft, vague questions elicit general, uninformative answers.

Arrive early. Introduce yourself and your purpose and express sincere thanks for the other's time. Ask permission before recording the conversation. Start the interview with general open-ended questions that also indicate you've done your research ("I noticed from your bio that you've held this position several years. I'm interested in how the progression of jobs you've had led to where you are now"). As the interview progresses, ask more detailed questions or probe for specific examples. At the end of the interview, have a planned final question ("I've gained a lot of useful information from our time today. Before we finish, I'd like to ask what advice you would give to someone in my position who wants to work in the public sector"). When interviewing potential employees, one might finish by asking, "What else do we need to know about you?" or "If you were hired for this position, what would you do on your first day?"

After the interview, process the notes, analyze the information, and send a thank you note or e-mail to the other person. In a job interview situation, there may be a company requirement to document the interview or to prepare formal evaluations of each candidate.

When conducting job interviews, meticulous detail is warranted. Hiring is an expensive and time-consuming enterprise. Detailed research on the technical skills and dispositions that will best fit the current team is a prudent step. Likewise, questions should be prepared that reveal the applicant's nature. In general, questions that ask for specific examples of what the applicant has done or how the applicant would manage a specific situation are more telling than very general questions. In addition, disclosing details about the job to applicants will assist them in determining their fitness for the position. ("You will be required to work closely with others on a team without much instruction or supervision. Can you describe a situation for me when you worked independently?") Interviews can educate others as well as provide information about them.

The Mirroring Interviewer Technique

Dreeke and Navarro (2009) argue that mirroring will elicit greater depth of disclosure because "people want to be communicated with as they like to communicate" (p. 6). While their conclusions focused on a law enforcement context, the same principles can be applied to any interview. By selecting the primary characteristics of a respondent, the interviewer knows whether to start with social chitchat or go directly to the meat of the issue. Table 4.3 presents the dimensions of communication that an interviewer can mirror.

Dreeke and Navarro argue that whether someone has a social versus task orientation and direct versus indirect style determines a person's preferred communication mode. Directors are task-oriented and direct. Thinkers are task-oriented and indirect. Relaters are socially oriented and

Table 4.3

Interview Communication Styles

People Oriented	Task Oriented
Relaxed	Formal
Likes to hear opinions	Focuses on facts
Shares feelings	Keeps feelings inside
Flexible about time	Rigid in use of time
Feels to decisions	Thinks to a decision
Spontaneous	Detailed planner

Direct	Indirect
Takes risks	Avoids risk
Quick decisions	Cautious decisions
Confrontational	Indirect about disagreement
Impatient	Easygoing
Talks and tells	Listens and asks
Outgoing	Reserved
Offers opinions	Keeps opinions private

indirect. Socializers are people-oriented and direct. Depending on the interviewer's knowledge of the individual or the interviewee's responses during the first few questions, the interviewer would switch to a style that mirrors the interviewee.

When communicating with Directors, be businesslike, present facts, demonstrate good organization, avoid repetition, emphasize results, and be precise. Thinkers expect the interviewer to be well-prepared, action-oriented, detailed, logical, and to have solid facts. Relaters prefer a warm climate and people who show an interest in them. Spend enough time for trust to develop, state disagreement in terms of feelings rather than facts, and apply collaborative listening skills. Socializers want the focus on themselves. Be supportive of their ideas, be upbeat, casual, and embrace their topic changes that may seem to go off topic.

Case: The Redevelopment Project

Rust Town is a Midwestern U.S. city with a population of 62,000. At one time, the city was a manufacturing center that hosted multiple paper mills and an auto body assembly plant. Most of these manufacturing facilities closed in the 1970s and 1980s, resulting in job losses and a drop in population from a high of 80,000 in 1975. Rust Town's unemployment rate has hovered at 5.75 percent and many of its neighborhoods are run down with older housing, abandoned lots, and overgrown weeds in public parks.

According to the recent census, the poverty rate was 22 percent. Whites comprised 81.9 percent of the population, blacks comprised 8.4 percent of the population, and 6.4 percent of the population was Hispanic.

The city partnered with a major hotel chain to redevelop an aging part of downtown for a hotel convention center and parking garage project. The redevelopment effort would result in the loss of six square blocks of existing downtown housing. The six blocks, located in an area the locals referred to as the second ward, was mostly older homes that had been subdivided into rental units, vacant lots where abandoned homes had been torn down, and the city's oldest Catholic church, built in 1850.

The mayor of Rust Town appeared with the CEO of the hotel chain, the president of the Chamber of Commerce, and other business leaders to announce the plans for the redevelopment project. Taken by surprise by the announcement, black ministers from the second ward and throughout the city held their own press conference the next day to denounce the project as an attempt by the city to "get rid of" black residents. The ministers planned a march on city hall for the next weekend.

After the mayor's news conference, the local historical society held an emergency board meeting to discuss strategies to protect and preserve the historic Catholic church located in the second ward.

Surveying the news articles and letters received about the project, the mayor approaches you, his assistant chief of staff, to help him address the suddenly complicated redevelopment project.

Discussion Questions

1. How would you suggest the mayor should proceed?
2. What steps are necessary to successfully resolve the conflict?
3. If you could have advised the mayor on this project three months earlier, what would you have advised that might have prevented the conflict?

5

Creating and Maintaining
Effective Work Relationships

How we speak with others and form relationships affects the quality
of work and our satisfaction with the work environment. Interpersonal
communication was one of three key dimensions in Pandey and Garnett's
(2006) model of public sector communication competence, along with
formal internal communication and external communication.

Relationships are built on personal and sometimes idiosyncratic connections. Good interpersonal relationships help motivate others to do
their best work. Coworkers with positive interpersonal interactions have
different experiences than those with negative dispositions. Supervisors
who have crafted shared experiences with their subordinates have more
communication choices than supervisors who remain aloof. A local
government employee who has a history of listening to citizen concerns
may have more congenial interactions than if the public employee is
perceived as a faceless bureaucrat.

The individual cost of poor interpersonal communication skills is
clear. Management trainers and consultants see patterns of interpersonal
behaviors in employees who seemed to have promising careers that
stopped short—including termination of someone who was selected
for advancement. These individuals share characteristics such as being
insensitive, competing too much, spending too much time isolated in
an office without interacting with others, advancing dictatorial orders,
sounding overly critical, being easily angered, behaving arrogantly, or
manipulating others (Chappelow and Leslie 2004). Any combination
of these interpersonal behaviors can derail a career or leave even a top
performer pushed to the sidelines going nowhere. Employers often seek
out applicants with good interpersonal skills. A survey of city managers
found that people skills were a main interest of employers when hiring
or promoting employees (Berman and West 2008).

Acquiring advanced interpersonal communication skills and developing emotional intelligence are important for all public sector employees. This chapter discusses interpersonal skills within several contexts experienced by supervisors and managers in the public sector, including performance reviews, motivating employees, and giving employee feedback. Before discussing how interpersonal communication skills impact specific work activities, the concept of emotional intelligence is introduced.

Emotional Intelligence and Emotional Labor

Many observers and scholars of human behavior have noted that some people seem to have an intuitive sense of how to relate to others and handle themselves in challenging situations. The term *emotional intelligence* came into use to describe these attributes. The division of personal capacities between intellectual and emotional intelligence is a relatively new concept. Intellectual intelligence connotes knowledge and logic ability. Emotional intelligence refers to self-awareness and social astuteness. When employees are promoted due to their technical or scientific competence, these new managers occasionally find their social skills are less robust than their intellectual abilities.

While authors may label the elements differently, emotional intelligence generally encompasses a mix of four components: self-awareness, managing emotions, recognition of emotion in others, and relationship skills (see, for example, Hughes, Patterson and, Terrell 2005; Hughes and Terrell 2007; Vigoda-Gadot and Meisler 2010; Wong and Law 2002).

Those labeled low in emotional intelligence are characterized by little awareness of personal emotions or how their behavior may affect others, difficulty in managing personal relationships, low self-motivation, and minimal skill in managing conflict—typically not the profile of successful managers. Greater emotional intelligence leads to enhanced choices for supervisors. For example, when an employee asks questions about a supervisor's instructions, someone low in emotional intelligence may react defensively. Individuals higher in emotional intelligence feel secure enough to manage challenges without extreme reactions.

Emotional intelligence characteristics are presented in Table 5.1. In general, self-confidence and a more positive outlook on life are helpful. The last item in Table 5.1 is of particular interest—happiness. Those who exhibit negativity are a black cloud in any situation. It may seem odd to say that it is more competent to *choose* happiness, but that is ex-

Table 5.1

Key Elements of Emotional Intelligence

1.	Self-regard	Increased feelings of self-confidence and decreased fear of failure
2.	Emotional self-awareness	Increased connectedness with personal feelings rather than actively suppressing feelings
3.	Assertiveness	Stating one's ideas or feelings with confidence rather than with aggression or passive-aggressiveness
4.	Independence	Comfort within the self rather than co-dependent
5.	Self-actualization	Comfort within self and others and works toward higher levels of self development
6.	Empathy	Understanding others' feelings without agreement or sympathy
7.	Social responsibility	Consideration of other's welfare as part of decisions rather than purely selfish reasoning
8.	Interpersonal relationships	Success at establishing and maintaining healthy personal relationships with others; balance of humility and friendship
9.	Stress tolerance	Confidence in oneself during times of stress compared to the angst felt by the insecure
10.	Impulse control	Acting because of choice rather than impulse
11.	Reality testing	Able to consider the consequences of actions and to put aside naive trust in others
12.	Flexibility	Confidence to work in contexts that are ambiguous, changing, or uncertain without undue stress
13.	Problem solving	Able to analyze and define issues
14.	Optimism	A view of the world that expects the best (while being able to handle the worst) rather than exhibiting doubt and negativity in response to every situation
15.	Happiness	Choosing to be happy regardless of the situation

Source: Adapted from Hughes, Patterson, and Terrell (2005).

actly the argument made by advocates of emotional intelligence. Social neuroscience may provide some support for these claims. Some studies show emotional signals can overwhelm the interpreter's view of a message. For example, neuroscientists have found that employees who get positive feedback in a negative or sarcastic tone can feel worse than the employee who gets negative feedback presented in a good-natured way (Goleman and Boyatzis 2008). Strategically selecting the right tone of voice is one way of demonstrating emotional intelligence when speaking with subordinates, coworkers, and the public.

The term *emotional labor* was coined to describe actions that are more difficult due to personal disposition (Ashkanasy, Zerbe, and Hartel 2002). Work can be draining when someone is required to do tasks that are outside his or her individual style, whether based on a Myers-Briggs type personality test or other personality frameworks. Some public sector jobs require empathy from a social service/crisis worker or a tough demeanor from police officers. Working with abused children may entail the emotional labor of not showing the horror one feels when hearing a child's story, as negative emotion can lead the child to believe he or she has done something wrong (Newman, Guy, and Mastracci 2009). First responders to accidents, 911 operators, and other professionals who interact with troubled individuals cannot be faint of heart. When emotional labor becomes too difficult, employees may harden their feelings as a self-protection mechanism. Hiring freezes and workforce cutbacks may exacerbate the effects of emotional labor burnout. Newman et al. (2009) argue that soft skills and emotional competence are key leadership skills and attributes for front line public employees: "Why should we care about emotional labor and the art of leadership? We suggest that the skills inherent in their practice are essential to—indeed, the essence of—service to the public" (p. 16).

Higher emotional intelligence among government workers is particularly important in situations that involve strong emotions, tasks that require coworker and stakeholder involvement, problem solving that requires creative thinking, or in organizations undergoing change (Berman and West 2008). Emotional intelligence is one component of a manager's ability to motivate others. The next section discusses interpersonal communication skills that relate to the motivation of employees, volunteers, and the general public.

Motivation and the Public Sector

Researchers seem convinced that charismatic leaders are the best motivators (Babcock-Roberson and Strickland 2010). Unfortunately, few individuals can bring the full force of charisma to their work. The majority of team leaders, supervisors, and agency managers must learn interpersonal skills to motivate employees and to avoid unnecessary alienation of the public.

A robust research literature tested numerous hypotheses about employee motivation and performance in the private and public sectors. No clear consensus emerged. The variables that impact employee motivation and performance are complex—including employee characteristics and perceptions of actions by upper management, human resources practices, and supervisor interpersonal behavior. At one level, employee motivation and performance is a mélange of things that may be out of the control of a given supervisor or agency head. For example, motivators can be extrinsic or intrinsic. Extrinsic motivators such as promotions, raises, bonuses, gifts, or job security guarantees might be provided by the organization, totally absent, or even illegal. When available to an agency, the extrinsic motivator may be fully funded or rarely funded. Intrinsic motivators are characteristics the employee brings to the workplace, such as ambition, trust, desire for meaningful work, or public service motivation. Managers with good interpersonal skills can cultivate intrinsic motivations if they understand the uniqueness of each employee. For example, supervisors' use of motivating language is related to reducing discretionary absenteeism (Mayfield and Mayfield 2009).

What Is Public Service Motivation?

Theory and research endorse the maxim that public sector employees are different from their private sector counterparts—they have intentionally chosen an occupation to match a desire to be of service, to make a difference in society, or to advance social justice for specific populations (Buelens and Van den Broeck 2007; Crewson 1997; and Wright 2007). Research tends to indicate that public sector employees (compared to the private sector) were less motivated by salary, more motivated by responsibility, desired supportive work climates more, needed high status less, and viewed their work as having high job security (Buelens and Van den Broeck 2007; Bright 2008; Frank and Lewis 2004; Wright 2001). The effects of public service motivation seem stronger in supervisors than lower level workers (Taylor and Taylor 2010). If an employee's motivation is intrinsic—a desire to be of service—the supervisor's level of sharing about that individual's personal contributions becomes very important. Taking the time to acknowledge the difference someone makes can be highly motivational.

In the past, polls indicated that public sector workers tried to do their best work, even when it interfered with the rest of their lives (Frank and Lewis 2004). Changing workforce dynamics and the economics of the twenty-first century are testing public service motivation. Some authors paint a dismal picture: "Years of bashing the bureaucrats, stingy legislatures, and employee cut-backs have resulted in an inhospitable work environment that discourages job applicants" (Hays and Sowa 2010, p. 100). When monetary incentives, cutbacks in budgets, contracting out services, loss of job security, or other factors increase workload, managers cannot trust public service motivation to buoy all employees through the tough times. Pandey (2010) expressed concern that budget cutbacks were a threat to public workers' perception of a social contract where job security was linked to less desirable workplace factors such as the acceptance of lower pay. A perceived or real loss of job security in public sector work may impact the workforce in unpredictable ways.

Supervisors and managers can use the strategies presented here to reinforce public service motivators through interpersonal actions. We focus primarily on interpersonal communication strategies because first-level supervisors rarely have control over agency policy on substantive rewards. In light of contradictory research about the efficacy of financial incentives, it is even more critical to understand intrinsic motivations. Perry, Mesch, and Paarlberg (2006) concluded that merit pay systems can be moderately effective in motivating performance, but feedback plus money and social recognition was better than money alone. Merit systems and pay-for-performance have not been successful in the public sector. Individual agencies rarely control all of the factors necessary for pay-for-performance work, such as adequate funding for merit pay raises, so the probability of success from purely economic strategies is low (Glassman et al. 2010).

Strategies to Buoy Employee Motivation

Recognition

Being recognized for excellence can support the intrinsic motivation of doing one's best or serving the public. When designing recognition programs, it is wise to analyze the specific workers, volunteers, or citizens who will be honored. While it is important to find a way to recognize every solid employee or volunteer, if awards are perceived as pro forma they will have less motivational impact. Likewise, individual recognition that runs counter to an organizational or cultural value of group equality may demotivate employees (a group award would be better). Table 5.2 presents several low-cost recognition options.

Employees and supervisors should understand how recognition might interface with evaluation processes. It requires interpersonal skill to honor an employee for an award on a short-term special project and at the same time remind the employee that work on their regular duties needs

Table 5.2

Low-Cost Recognition Options

•	Unexpected Rewards	Food treats or small gift cards delivered by the supervisor with some words of encouragement or praise.
•	Spontaneous Award Decorations	Supervisor/manager prepares a "kit" of festive decorations to adorn an employee's cubicle to recognize an achievement.
•	Personal Congratulations	For employee of the month or similar high-profile awards without monetary components, every supervisor in the unit appears on the day of the award to congratulate the employee.
•	Other Resources for Awards	If allowed by agency rules, time off with pay or extra training can be a valued reward.
•	Personal Notes	Managers can write personal notes to congratulate an employee on an award or particularly meritorious work on a project.
•	Photos	Recognize work efforts by posting a photo of the group or featuring the team in an internal newsletter.
•	Photo Collage	Display a collage of photos showing everyone who worked on a project or contributed to success during the year.
•	Today's Star	Create an award that can be given the same day to an employee who manages a particularly difficult situation well.

to be improved. If an employee has substandard performance overall, any award should be contextualized for the employee (i.e., an award for exceptional work on one project should be perceived as encouragement for continued good work in the future rather than as erasing a poor overall, annual performance).

Job Design

If the employee is motivated intrinsically, designing the job to fit the individual's skills can positively affect absenteeism, turnover, organizational commitment, productivity, and job satisfaction (Perry, Mesch, and Paarlberg 2006). The implication of this research is that otherwise solid and motivated employees who are in a job that doesn't fit may be transformed into more productive employees when their job specifications are altered to match their skills. Since each employee may find different aspects of work meaningful, job design as a motivation strategy should be customized for each employee. While rigid federal and state job clas-

Table 5.3

Ideas to Use Training as a Motivational Incentive

- Reserve some training money as a unique reward for valued employees.
- Package training available to all employees into themed certificates that count toward bonuses, promotions, or raises.
- Provide time off to compensate employees who attend trainings from a pre-approved list.
- To enliven the work environment, use job cross-training as an opportunity for highly motivated, competent employees.
- Create supervision or management internship or mentoring opportunities as rewards for individuals who complete specific training courses aimed at management development for future leaders.
- Pay for college credit in approved programs.

sification systems or union contracts may make this strategy impossible, when policies allow, cross-training or other job design strategies can be useful motivational tools.

Training

Offering employees training can be a motivator (Fernandez and Moldogaziev 2011). Interestingly, organizations that offer training equitably to all employees may benefit from an overall increase in workforce competence but lose individual motivational value (Whitener 2001). If this phenomenon holds true for the public sector as well as the private, managers might strategically hold back some training opportunities for special incentives. Table 5.3 identifies several ways to use training as a motivational tool. As with all other ideas in this book, agency rules and policies should be examined before implementing any new strategy.

To realize the full impact of a strategy, such as offering training as a motivator, an interpersonally astute supervisor will explain that the opportunity is linked to the agency's perception of the worker as one who is making a valuable contribution. The manner in which motivational strategies are contextualized can be equally important or even more important than the reward itself.

Trust and Commitment from the Organization

Trust is a fuzzy concept that may mean different things to different people. Even so a trustworthy supervisor or organization can be a motivating force. Many factors affect whether employees trust their employers. "Individuals do not come up to organizations as blank slates when it comes to trust. They bring attitudes and predispositions from every sector of their lives, born of their experiences at work and an overall predisposition about how they will deal with others" (Carnevale and Ham 2010, p. 267). If employees believe the organization is committed to them, they in turn have greater trust in and commitment to the organization (Whitener 2001). Thomas, Zolin, and Hartman elaborate on the value of trust:

> [An employee who believes] her supervisor will treat her fairly, provide opportunities for professional growth, make sure she has the necessary tools to do her work well, and provide good guidance [will perform better]. If these expectations are met, the employee is more likely to focus full attention on her work tasks. Conversely, if the employee distrusts her supervisor, she is more likely to spend time covering her back, questioning her boss's directions, or even looking for another job. (2009, p. 290)

While supervisors may have little control over organizational policies and upper management behaviors, they can use interpersonal communication to build a trusting relationship with subordinates or volunteers. A study of federal workers indicated employees expect leaders to have strong interpersonal skills and show benevolence, honesty, and integrity (Yang and Kassekert 2009). Trust is fostered through consistent behaviors and sophisticated interpersonal communication.

Trust and commitment may be even more important in nonprofit organizations. Volunteers view commitment as a two-way street: the volunteer is committed to the organization and thinks the organization should be committed to the volunteer. Table 5.4 presents several strategies to foster trust among coworkers and volunteers.

Humane Performance Reviews

Formal and informal reviews of employee performance are part and parcel of supervision. There are many ways to conduct a performance review (discussed in Human Resources courses). Regardless of the formal structure mandated at a specific agency, the manner in which a supervisor phrases feedback and conducts reviews has a pervasive impact. Is the feedback timely? Does the supervisor seem comfortable and honest when delivering the feedback or conducting a performance review? Is the feedback helpful to the employee and the organization? Are goals clear or fuzzy? Interpersonal skills and emotional intelligence are required

Table 5.4

Strategies to Foster Trust

- Drop by to say hello to an employee when you don't have any other objective.
- Privately keep track of which employees/volunteers receive praise or awards and look for opportunities to say something positive to those whose efforts might be overlooked. Everyone needs encouragement.
- Create a non-threatening way for management to respond honestly to rumors— spend five minutes at a staff meeting on items drawn from a rumor basket.
- Encourage supervisors who are not close to their staff/volunteers to find ways to have conversations with staff and work toward better relationships.
- Use employees' names when speaking with them.
- For those who must work on holidays, managers can show up with treats.
- Executives could meet for coffee with randomly selected employees once a month.
- Be consistent over time in enforcing policies.
- Avoid saying one thing and doing another.
- Ask employees what their concerns are and what motivates them to do their jobs well.
- Give employees accurate information before rumors start.
- Create an environment where employees feel safe to express opinions.

to strike the right tone when delivering either praise or suggestions to correct substandard behavior.

Positive feedback is intended to motivate and reinforce productive behavior with the idea that employees will sustain or improve their efforts. Negative feedback is intended to identify errors in work with the idea that information will improve performance (Cianci, Klein, and Seijts 2010). About one-third of supervisors are required to deliver a poor performance review to an employee at some point (Daley 2008). Unfortunately an evaluation session can go awry due to poor supervisor communication. Without strategic skillfulness during the delivery of bad news, employee motivation can be ruined, supervisor self-esteem can be hurt, general workplace communication climate can be poisoned, and procedures can be broken.

Performance reviews can focus on many things. The structure of an agency's review process may lean in a variety of philosophical directions. For example, there are two kinds of employee-centered goals: learning and performance. Learning goals encompass new information, skills, or being exposed to learning experiences (e.g., "In the next three months, I will attend a software training session"). Performance goals seek skill competence ("At the end of three months, I will be able to use the new software error free").

Table 5.5

Goal Setting

- Set smaller goals with regular review rather than larger goals with longer time frames.
- Use part of the regular staff meeting agenda to talk about a specific unit goal and the progress/challenges the unit is facing.
- When possible, set goals that create a sense of accomplishment for employees (as opposed to goals that cannot be implemented easily as the procedures or resources are outside the employee's power to control).
- Only set goals that are important or are directly linked to accomplishment of the organizational mission.
- Explain the importance of specific goals.

How employees interpret the message delivered during a performance review is strongly influenced by interpersonal factors. Performance feedback is perceived as fair if it is clear and unambiguous to the employee and not open to interpretation, the delivery of the message demonstrated constructive concern for the subordinate, the person delivering the feedback showed awareness of the specifics of the job conditions, and policies are applied consistently in the organization (Chory and Westerman 2009).

Goal Setting

Many performance evaluation systems require regularly scheduled goal-setting exercises for individual employees or units. Some approaches foster control systems, such as rules, sanctions, monitoring, and rewards based on production, and others are commitment systems, which encourage employees to identify with the organization's goals so they want to be productive and effective (Whitener 2001). When employees understand and buy into the importance of organizational goals, they may be more committed. Managers should seek goal commitment to ensure that employees actively work toward unit objectives and are motivated to persevere when obstacles arise. For supervisors who have interpersonal skills, these conversations can occur on a regular basis as well as be a part of scheduled performance appraisal meetings. Supervisors with low emotional intelligence may overlook the value of discussing goals. Research indicates that reasonable goals positively impact performance at all levels of the organization. However, when goals are confusing,

---

Insights from the Field
Telling the Employee about Inappropriate Behavior

A State of Nevada Human Resources Officer

If nobody tells you that what you're doing is inappropriate or that it's affecting somebody, how would you know to change your behavior? Sometimes we have managers that let employees continue misbehaving. And it gets significantly worse. Then finally something blows up and they want to suspend them or fire them right there and then. We say, you never told the employee up to this point that what they were doing was inappropriate. So why would you think that they would change behavior? If you didn't tell them to stop, what was your role in that?

---

the reverse occurs. If goals are too complex or employees fear the goal, performance may decrease (Perry, Mesch, and Paarlberg 2006).

Goal Management

In the public sector, goals inherently are difficult to manage, as there may be a weak link between individual actions and outcomes. Van Wart (2011) argues it is best to set goals around outcomes rather than processes whenever possible. However, some employee's jobs may entail more process than product. In these cases, it can be unfair to evaluate an employee only on a part of his or her job just because one part is easier to objectively measure.

Goals also may be imposed on agencies by external sources. Even so, as Wright (2007) concluded, public sector managers should "take care to assign performance expectations in ways that not only clearly explain what employees should do and how they should do it but also *why* they should do it. Such communication is important in facilitating employee work motivation" (p. 60).

Communicative strategy when evaluating or discussing goals is important. Employees who are at the top of the evaluation matrix may experience too much focus on their one area of weakness. Since everything else is good, the supervisor sometimes spends the entire session on the one area that could be improved. While the proportion of the employee's work is excellent, the majority of the conversation is about the minority that needs improvement. Emphasizing only items needing improvement is called the weakness trap. Evaluators should consider the importance of each area of evaluation when deciding how much attention to focus on a strength or weakness. Markle (2010) advises focusing on strengths.

If improvement is critical to the job, document the insufficiency, shorten the time frame between evaluation sessions, and provide necessary coaching/training. By shortening the time between assessments, everyone maintains focus on the job. If improvements do not occur, there are documented reasons to follow policies toward termination. If a volunteer is not able to perform the required duties, a volunteer coordinator can find another way the individual can be of service.

Telling employees during a down economy that "they should just be happy to have a job" can demotivate long-term loyalty. Even if this type of comment is true, it is unnecessary. Likewise, a supervisor who uses a verbally aggressive style to foster employee improvement sends a mixed message. For example, mentoring a new worker using verbally aggressive and negative language rarely will have beneficial results (Madlock and Kennedy-Lightsey 2010).

Interpersonal Communication Competence

Performance appraisals and goal setting are specific activities completed by most agencies or nonprofit organizations. Interpersonal communication competence and acting strategically from insights gained from emotional intelligence are important to the choices managers make every day. The following section investigates choices managers can make to foster better communication throughout the organization.

Sharing Information and Including Employees

It is not uncommon for bosses to attend strategy meetings with their peers and convey none of that information to subordinates. Likewise, many managers will work with their superiors to make changes in work processes without asking for input from those who will be putting the changes into practice. While research has not linked including employees in organizational processes with increased performance, asking employees for input does seem related to organizational loyalty and job satisfaction (Perry, Mesch, and Paarlberg 2006). Organizational expert Peter Block commented on why accountability is best when chosen rather than just

---

Table 5.6

Strategies to Foster Employee Inclusion

- Communicate information that can be shared about higher level goal planning or problem solving (as opposed to waiting until issues are resolved).
- Ask employees their opinions (as opposed to only telling them the results of decisions).
- Keep a verbal communication channel open between supervisors/managers and employees (as opposed to a closed door or unavailable manager).
- Create at least one channel of continuous employee feedback to management.

---

imposed: "I'll only care for what I own. And I will only really care for what I've helped create. It gives me an emotional stake in the future if I feel the future is mine to create rather than yours or theirs to create. And most of us defend against the future created by others and against the idea that someone else knows what's best and we don't" (quoted in Rush 2004, p. 24). An indirect benefit may accrue from including employees in organizational processes: "the greatest organizational gains from employee participation may come from producing *better* decisions. . . . In the process, individuals who might not normally share information may do so, including employees at various levels in the hierarchy" (Perry, Mesch, and Paarlberg 2006, p. 509).

Another important aspect of sharing information with employees is what happens when information is not shared. Human beings hate an information vacuum. Lacking information from the organization, employees will fill the empty space with rumor, speculation, and anxiety. Not only does speculation create errors, it takes a considerable amount of energy from other work activities. During times of flux, holding information too close to the vest often is not the best plan. Building the kind of work relationships in which subordinates trust that a manager will share information (that is legal to share and within policy) will reduce employee anxiety and prevent some manifestations of workplace conflict.

Managing Expectations

Excellence comes not only from making the right choices, but also in having others see actions in the way they were intended. When we do not share information to contextualize a situation, others are free to invent their own views of reality. Interpersonal skills are important to align viewpoints and contain speculation.

Public employees and leaders must gain interpersonal communication competence and put effort into expectancy management, or framing how others perceive actions. In some cases, employee and public expectation about how a decision is made may be more important than the actual decision. For example, if employees become accustomed to being consulted about decisions but the manager needs to make a quick decision due to statutory or timing constraints, employees may misperceive the manager's unilateral decision as an inappropriate usurpation of their right to be included. Discord, and perhaps resistance to the decision, will result. To frame the situation and manage expectations, the supervisor might explain the exigency and the quick timeline when informing employees about the action. Likewise, if the public perceives a meeting as seeking their input when in actuality decisions already have been made, mismanagement of their expectations may lead to public outcry.

Active expectancy management requires forethought about goals and sharing information about the processes that will be used. In addition, interested parties need to be provided a reasonable rationale on how decisions will be made in each instance, as well as why a particular method is being used. Disclosure of information about processes, decision modes, and who the decision makers are separates arguments about how to decide from disagreements about what the decision should be.

In the context of performance appraisals, it is not enough that a supervisor behave appropriately; employees must perceive that the supervisor's decisions and actions are appropriate. When agency personnel do not work to frame issues and manage expectations, rumor or innuendo may rule the day. "Mistreatment in the workplace is when an employee believes that he or she has not been treated fairly in the course of performing his or her job" (Olson-Buchanan and Boswell 2009, p. 1), such as the belief that one's performance evaluation was unfair, raises or promotions were given to others due to favoritism, clients or managers behave badly, or other employees are not treating them well. The belief that one is being mistreated (whether or not the belief is accurate) results in lower morale and less efficient workplace behaviors. It may also result in slacking, retaliation, turnover, grievances, and lawsuits (Olson-Buchanan and Boswell 2009). In some cases, these feelings of mistreatment arise from situations in which supervisors have not shared enough information about the context, criteria were not transparent, or mistrust was allowed to grow.

Any behavior that is outside what another person anticipates in a specific context may create an expectancy violation. For example, swearing is not expected in formal situations (Johnson and Lewis 2010). Profanity and an array of other behaviors may be shocking when enacted by a high-ranking public manager or by public employees in a formal setting. Unless chosen for strategic reasons, public employees should use positive rather than negative speech strategies. It is better to instruct a subordinate on how to do a job correctly than to yell at someone for being stupid.

Expectancy management also can relate to work sequencing. Managers who explain goals and priorities may help motivate employees whose innate sense of prioritization may differ from the supervisors' view (Farmer and Seers 2004). For example, an employee may value closure and thus will complete a file entirely before passing it to the next employee. However, the next employee to receive the file may only need a portion of the information. Discussions about workflow could reframe the closure-focused employee's perspective. Likewise, if expectations are not managed about what should be done first or how the public should be treated, employees will implement their individual personal style preferences. The place to start on employee expectation management is when the employee is hired.

Motivating Across Generational Lines

Studies consistently find differences in work behaviors across generational lines. For example, older employees work harder than their younger counterparts and have greater public service motivation (Frank and Lewis 2004; Vandenabeele 2011). Workers from each generation require different motivational strategies (see Table 5.7). A supervisor's approach to each age group may need customization. Customization of communication should not be confused with favoritism. Each employee should receive appropriate motivating attention from the supervisor. Adapting strategy to fit the employee may be more desirable than using exactly the same words with everyone. Behaviors that motivate one age group may demotivate another. Younger employees may perceive their casual work behaviors as appropriate and justified; bosses from other generations may perceive these actions as insubordination. Cole (2008a, 2008b) found younger employees perceive corrective actions based on insubordination as extremely unfair.

It may be useful to talk about how members of different generations prefer to work and interact with each other. For example, millennials

Table 5.7

Adapting to Various Generations

Veteran Generation: Born 1920–1940
- Prefer a more relaxed pace
- May be more comfortable with formal titles and formal speech

Boomers: Born 1940–1960
- Prefer personal greetings by name
- Are comfortable when bosses drop in to see how they are doing
- May like the identity of being a "regular" citizen-visitor to the agency
- Team oriented and loyal to employer

Gen Xers: Born 1960–1980
- Efficiency and on-task may be more important than work relationships
- Like to ask many questions and challenge past ideas; need to understand why tasks are important
- Like to work independently
- Want upper management to listen to their ideas
- Want quick feedback
- May want to be anonymous and invest little energy in work
- Distrustful of policies

Millennials: Born 1980–2000
- Want to be respected regardless of experience level
- Like to be entertained
- Believe they can be efficient multitaskers
- Have a wide range of friends via social media with whom they are in continuous contact
- Blend work and social life

Source: Adapted from Poindexter (2008); Raines and Hunt (2000).

may underestimate the value of face-to-face contact and interpersonal communication (Hartman and McCambridge 2011). A supervisor who is aware of generational differences has more options when motivating individuals and asking workers to adopt the culture of the organization. Generational differences is another arena where managing expectations about workplace behavior is important.

Demotivators: The Dark Side of Interpersonal Communication

While managers can motivate employees by using positive interpersonal communication strategies, it is equally important to avoid behaviors that demotivate. Whether directed at employees or the public, some behaviors can make relationships worse and goal accomplishment more difficult. Demotivators can occur simply because public employees have not thought through the potential consequences of their communication or lack thereof. Halachmi and van der Krogt (2010) claim supervisor "violation of an employee's sense of fairness, justice, or equity" is the largest workplace demotivator (p. 552). For example, casual or laissez faire management can lead to inconsistencies and workplace misbehavior, which may precipitate high turnover. Kim and Lee (2007) explain: "High turnover not only damages employee morale, because of the increased workload for remaining workers, but also compromises the quality of services that directly affect clients' welfare" (p. 228).

Halachmi and van der Krogt's study underscores the need for supervisors with good interpersonal communication skills and emotional intelligence. It is the employee's "sense of fairness, justice, or equity" that makes a difference in how a supervisor's actions are perceived. Even so, perception is a slippery phenomenon. There is no guarantee that supervisors with excellent interpersonal communication can control employee perceptions. Not developing personal contact with employees or attempting to manage expectations, however, leaves how efforts are perceived entirely to other people's imaginative discretion.

Managing employee perceptions around evaluation, policies, grievances, raises, and promotions is important if morale and productivity are to be maximized. The potential for misinterpretation is high. Managers believe their disciplinary actions are fair, but more than 50 percent of those disciplined believe the opposite (Atwater, Brett, and Charles 2007).

Whenever a supervisor takes an action or conveys a decision without attempting to control how that decision is interpreted, perceptual mischief is possible. Humans will fit information into patterns and make inferences based on few, if any, facts to create a reality that makes sense to them. Lacking other contextualization, an employee may see a procedural change as retaliation by a supervisor. Without framing by the supervisor, it is easier for employees to see a new policy as management abuse. When criteria for promotions are not transparent, those not selected may infer they were discriminated against because of their age, sex, or race. Daley's (2007) research indicates, "employees form an image of the organization from how well it handles the grievance and disciplinary process. The sense of protection or fear that grievance and disciplinary systems engender can have a major impact" (p. 282).

Specifically, when an employee felt misled or misused by the grievance system or was afraid to file a grievance, psychological withdrawal from the agency and coworkers often occurred. When employees withdraw, they are demotivated and may infect others in the agency or community with their disaffection.

> **Factoid:**   A new term has been added to our lexicon, *dooced*: "To be fired because of comments made about the company by an employee on a personal blog." (Atwater, Brett, and Charles 2007, p. 394)

Saying "No" Badly

It is easier to say "yes" to a request or deliver good news than to say "no" or deliver bad news. In *The Power of a Positive No*, Ury (2007) talks about the contrast between the pleasure of helping someone (saying "yes") and the discomfort of denying someone (saying "no"). Public sector employees may be in the business of saying "no" in many situations: to requests for special treatment, to requests to share information that must be held confidential by law, or to accept responses after an appeal time frame has passed. Denying a request is an exercise of power that may be required by statute. These conversations with the public are uncomfortable. The interpersonally competent individual explains the "no" in as gracious a manner as possible and strives to maintain a positive relationship.

Those who are more competent at interpersonal communication and have greater emotional intelligence have more options when saying "no." A small-minded individual may subvert the organizational responsibility of saying "no" into an opportunity to demean others ("You should have followed the rules" or "You should have submitted your appeal in on time").

Others who are not comfortable when they cannot immediately help a client may overcompensate by trying to be too nice. Saying "yes" when statutes require a "no" is inappropriate and will make matters worse in the long run. Likewise, minimizing the scope of a difficulty or unrealistically implying the situation will "work itself out" are not helpful responses. When giving bad news, the best policy is to be truthful without being brutal: "The deadline for this process has passed. The next option that you have is to appeal the deadline. Here are the rules for filing that ap-

Table 5.8

Saying "No" Gracefully

Comment:	Will you bring your famous homemade chili to the potluck this Friday?
Response:	*I would prefer to bring the sodas this time.*
Comment:	Can you get me this report right away?
Response:	*I'm finishing a task for the manager. I can get the report this afternoon after I turn in the task I'm working on.*
Comment:	Are you going to the lunch at noon today?
Response:	*I'll see you later at the 2 pm meeting. (The "No" is implied.)*
Comment:	Will you take my shift today at noon?
Response:	*Not today. If you ask me a day or so in advance we might be able to work out a trade of shifts.*

Source: Adapted from Ury (2007).

peal." In selecting the words to use, focus on the process rather than the person ("the application" rather than "your late application").

When saying "no" to a coworker, a modified strategy is recommended. Be clear and take responsibility for your decision. If a coworker repeatedly asks you to take a shift at lunch for reasons that you don't find credible, Ury recommends being clear without actually using the word "no," as it seems to activate defensive reactions. When asked, "Can you take my shift at lunch today?" respond with: "Hold on, that doesn't work for me. You'll have to work something else out." Table 5.8 details other ways to say "no."

Ury also recommends changing use of the word "but" to "and." For example, in response to a complaint about an increase in fees one's response could sound defensive or explanatory. Saying, "We raised fees, but we added more hours" sounds defensive. Replying to a question about a fee increase that sounds more explanatory might be phrased as, "We did raise fees, and we expanded hours so people can come in after regular work hours."

The positive interpersonal strategies discussed in this chapter and Ury's specific recommendations about phrasing denials share the common characteristic of respecting the other individual. Ury points out that 2,500 years ago Sun Tzu counseled warriors to build a golden bridge for opponents to retreat across rather than destroying them completely.

Today the golden bridge helps others maintain self-respect and reduce defensiveness, which in turn allow a positive relationship.

Giving bad news is acknowledged as one of the most difficult management tasks. Without the appropriate training, supervisors may ignore the need to give feedback, bungle the job, or feel betrayed by the organization because of their lack of skill. Tone is just as important as content when giving negative feedback if the supervisor is to be perceived as fair. Generally, feedback that is specific and includes the recipient in a discussion of remedies is most effective—"people believe they are entitled to 'have a say'" (Lizzio, Wilson, and MacKay 2008, p. 920). Simply asking for the recipient's perspective can help. "Please tell me what the situation looks like from your viewpoint." "What ideas do you have on how this situation can be improved?" Even bad news can be framed to the organization's advantage. Supervisors who have a large range of interpersonal skills can mitigate the defensive reactions inherent in bad news situations.

Factoid: *Sandwiching* is not an effective feedback strategy (a big slab of criticism sandwiched between two pieces of faint praise).

The Art of Giving Feedback

The feedback people receive can encourage more productive behaviors, perpetuate bad behavior, or cause additional problems. For example, when an employee arrives late, ignoring the behavior can be interpreted by the tardy worker as implied approval—being on time is not important. Feedback delivered by yelling or berating the employee in front of others demotivates. Telling the employee at an appropriate, private moment that being on time is important delivers the message that the supervisor is on top of what happens in the unit, is reasonable, and tardiness is not acceptable. Similarly, the feedback members of the public receive is important in establishing an agency's reputation.

Learning how to give appropriate, timely, feedback is a useful people skill—the higher one rises in the ranks of management, the more important the skill. For beginners, a structured system may be helpful. The four-step system presented in the skill development box (see p. 78) provides a structure to guide feedback. By memorizing what one will say

---

Skill Development
Four-Step Feedback

1. State one, recent behavior

Right: "This morning I noticed you arrived at work at 8:30 instead of 8:00."
Wrong: "You always are late."

2. Relate the detrimental effect of the behavior on the workplace

Right: "As a result, people were waiting in the lobby to be helped."
Wrong: "Everything got screwed up."

3. Describe the behavior you want to occur

Right: "I need you to be here at 8 every day or call in advance."
Wrong: "Don't mess up again."

4. Ask for agreement

Right: "Can you do that?"
Wrong: "You won't let me down, will you?"

---

in advance, the supervisor avoids several feedback traps: being vague, talking about personality characteristics rather than behaviors, sounding sarcastic, being demeaning, talking too long, or allowing the employee to sidetrack the conversation. Step 4 is important to allow the employee to clarify the situation or negotiate outcomes.

When dealing with employees and the public, remember that individuals process information differently and not everyone will understand or appreciate feedback in the same way. Some will misinterpret even the kindest intentions; others may become emotional or feel attacked. Return to check the other person's understanding of your intent after he or she has had time to assimilate the message. Sometimes engaging the other person in solving a problem may be a more successful strategy than any prepackaged feedback technique. Weitzel's (2004) comment on ineffective feedback in the business world is equally true in the public sector. Common mistakes include the following:

1. Expressing judgments ("You are a bad worker; "Your behavior is unacceptable") rather than descriptions ("When you are late, it slows down the project completion").
2. Being vague ("You should try to do a better job").
3. Implying threats inappropriately ("Something bad will happen if you don't get with the program").
4. Using aggressive humor ("I'd like to hit you for that comment, but policy doesn't allow it. Ha. Ha.").

Tables 5.9 and 5.10 identify criteria and strategic phrasing for feedback.

Another useful tool for giving feedback or seeking clarity is the sincerely curious question. Rather than assuming knowledge of another person's intention, be curious about what was meant. Instead of becoming defensive when strong or unusual language is used, be curious about how the other person interprets the situation. When using the technique illustrated in Table 5.11, it important to use a curious tone of voice rather than an evaluative or defensive tone.

Case: When Generations Collide

Dakota is a new employee in a New England area state department of transportation. She is eager to put her recent civil engineering degree

---

Table 5.9

Effective Feedback

- Focuses on behavior instead of personality
- Speaks of observed behaviors rather than inferred events or rumor
- Describes behaviors rather than judges or belittles
- Provides feedback sooner rather than later
- Asks the person with the undesired behavior for his or her ideas on better behavior or solutions
- Details the desired new behavior
- Sets attainable levels of expectation
- Gives the other person a chance to respond (without letting their excuses derail the conversation)
- Is delivered in a professional tone
- Comments on what has been observed. "You say everything is fine, but you don't look fine to me. What is going on?"
- Predicts consequences if behavior is not corrected or improvement goals are not met

Table 5.10

Crafting Appropriate Feedback

Less productively phrased comment	More productively phrased comment
You always try to make me look bad.	In the meeting, I felt belittled when you called my idea stupid.
You make me angry.	I feel angry right now.
You can't handle authority.	Let's talk about who has what role on this project.
You never let me help.	I would like to help on the next project.
Well done on that report.	The Maxwell report was excellent—It was well written and all the important facts were in the executive summary.
Why are you so stupid?	What were you thinking when you chose that action?
If you'd taken the time to read the instructions, you'd know.	That deadline has passed; let me give you the instructions for the late appeal process.
Why did you do that?	I'm curious about what led you to that choice.
Why are you always late?	Could you get to the meeting at 11 when it starts tomorrow?
We all think you are too sloppy in writing the reports.	I have concerns with your last report. Can we chat about the format you are using?

and minor in urban planning to work. She is assigned to the team of Mac Strong, a hard-driving manager known for his brusque attitude and dedication to bringing projects in on time. At Dakota's initial staff meeting, Mac hands her a stack of blueprints and planning folios and barks out, "I want your reviews of those plans on my desk by next Friday." The next day, Dakota knocks on Max's door and says, "I have evaluated this first plan and wanted to show you my results."

"You did them all already?" Mac asked incredulously. "No," Dakota stammered, "just this one."

"I ain't got time for that" Mac says with a dismissive wave of his hand. "Come back when you've got them all done."

Later, over a beer with his friends, Mac complains, "I got some young girl working for me but I don't know if she's going to make it. She keeps wasting my time! These kids expect me to be holding their hand through every step of the job!"

Table 5.11

Sincerely Curious Questions

- Ask a sincerely curious question about a word or concept.
  - ✓ "What do you mean by the word _____?"
- Ask a sincerely curious question about what you think the other is assuming.
  - ✓ "Do you think that this rule is unusual?"
  - ✓ "Did you really think I welcomed your trying to take over chairing the meeting?"
- Ask a sincerely curious question about the person's intentions
  - ✓ "I'm a bit hurt by your comment that I'm not being fair. What was your intention in saying that?"

Discussion Question

1. How might generational differences explain the dynamic between Dakota and Mac?

6

Working Together:
Meetings, Teams, and Parliamentary Procedure

Public employees and supervisors need the equivalent group management skills as private sector workers and the ability to manage public meetings. This chapter introduces theory and skills for effective meeting management, team building, and a beginner's view of parliamentary procedure—the rules that guide many commissions and formal policy groups.

While leadership sometimes is considered only a function of upper management, groups at all organizational levels need a guiding hand. Supervising employees, heading an interagency task force, or being the lead on a project are examples of situations in which knowledge of group behavior and leadership are useful. We begin with a discussion of how group skills and leadership apply to interagency relationships.

Collaborating Across Agencies

Public sector employees often must partner with others because jurisdictions may have overlapping responsibilities and multiple state, federal, business, or nonprofit entities face similar challenges. Cross-agency collaboration is a modern necessity (Thomson and Perry 2006). Agencies now recognize that thorny issues cross agency boundaries and cannot be solved through one entity's narrow mandate. Information, staff, or responsibility may need to be shared to ensure public safety, manage environmental issues, or respond to emergencies.

Organizational leadership expert Russ Linden (2012) identified three sources of interagency collaboration: bottom-up (employees create partnerships to facilitate their work), top-down (leaders formally create cross-agency teams), and crisis (an emergency forces collaborative efforts). Every government entity probably has many examples of successful interagency collaborative efforts. They also probably have examples of good ideas for collaboration that ended in political turf wars or personal power infighting. Table 6.1 shows Linden's six characteristics of successful collaborative efforts.

Table 6.1

Characteristics of Successful Interagency Collaboration

1. A specific, shared purpose that no agency can accomplish alone.
2. A willingness of each agency to contribute something to the goal (equipment, staff, expertise, funding).
3. The right people included in the collaborative effort (having both enough influence and enough stake in the outcome).
4. An open process for working together across organizational cultures.
5. A champion for the effort (with clout and passion for the issue).
6. Open, trusting relationships among the principals.

Being an Effective Intergovernmental Collaborator
Recommended Tips

Very few governmental programs are implemented in isolation. Most agencies and units of government are involved in a complicated set of intergovernmental partnerships. In this time of shrinking budgets and heightened expectations, knowing how to collaborate effectively is more critical than ever before.

1. Understand the time horizon of all the actors.

Each person in an intergovernmental collaboration will have different time horizons that impact their decisions, their willingness to collaborate, and their sense of urgency. Understanding how the other participants' time frames impact their behavior and willingness to cooperate is critical.

Let's take the first example of a time frame: term of office. If you are working with elected or appointed officials they are likely to be very sensitive to where they are in their term of office. At the beginning of a term of office, an official might be very anxious to show quick progress to impress the voters who elected them that they are working on the issues they promised. At the end of a term of office, on the other hand, an official might become quite cautious in your collaboration because they are fearful of the impact of the collaboration on their reelection efforts.

A similar dynamic applies to those who are appointed to their positions. They may be removed or reaffirmed by the elected official who put them in office based on the success or failure of your collaboration. Other potential collaborators may also be moved by time frame. For example, the director of a nonprofit may be appointed and reappointed on a yearly basis by a Board of Directors. Naturally, such a director may be sensitive to how news of your collaboration and its success or failure may impact their appointment or reappointment.

Long-term civil service employees, on the other hand, may have the luxury of planning many years in the future. Combining sensitivity to the ways in which all of these different terms of office impact perspective and willingness to collaborate is a critical part of being an effective intergovernmental collaborator.

2. Understand the fiscal constraints of all the actors.

Every organization has its own peculiarities to its budget and the restraints on the way in which it can use its budgets. Public sector agencies operate within a highly transparent environment. Public budgets are developed with public input and participation and all aspects of their budgets are open to public scrutiny including individual salaries. Nonprofit and corporate entities do not have this level of transparency with their budgets. Learning to work within the highly transparent public sector environment can be a struggle for these nonprofit and corporate partners in an intergovernmental collaboration. This difference may translate to a lack of the quality in the way in which information is shared and distributed among the partners.

Setting up the ground rules about how the extra burdens of public sector transparency will impact the project's budget transparency at the beginning of the project will benefit everyone. Another aspect to fiscal constraints in the public sector is the various rules that apply to how different "funds" can be used. For example, public sector agencies frequently utilize "dedicated funds" that have restrictions on how that money may be used. Dedicated funds cannot be shifted from one use to another. In budgeting terminology this is called fungibility. Public sector funds often lack fungibility. This lack of flexibility in the movement of money can be confusing to nonprofit and corporate sector partners. Another example of fiscal constraints is the requirements that attach to the receipt of certain kinds of federal grant monies.

A nonprofit that depends upon grant money may be highly sensitive to the federal "strings" attached to their funding. These restraints may limit the types of activities, partnerships, and expenses that each type of partner in the collaboration can participate in funding. Understanding these restraints that shape the collaboration will make each partner more effective in finding the best way to make common cause.

3. Understand the mission and values of the other actors in the collaboration.

Some common value or vision has brought all of you to the table to discuss or implement the collaboration in which you are involved. It is unlikely, however, that your mission completely overlaps with the mission of the other actors in the partnership. In fact, you would be missing many opportunities for collaboration if you limited yourself to only those agencies and partners with whom you are certain you share a common mission and value. It is not necessary for everyone to agree on a common mission. It is necessary, however, that you understand enough about the mission and values of the other actors in the partnership that you understand how their mission shapes their behaviors in the collaboration.

For example, let's assume we are working in a collaboration involving a city that has received federal funding to provide shelter for the homeless and a nonprofit. The nonprofit that runs the shelter is a religious organization whose mission is to provide spiritual counseling and salvation for its client. As the city works to comply with federal reporting requirements, it may request that the religious organization collect certain information about the clients in the shelter as well as information about what happens to them after they leave the shelter. The religious organization may resist this type of reporting as their priority is the spiritual health of the clients, not accountability as understood by a federal grant requirement. As such, they may not even collect the names of clients or routinely participate in follow-up data collection. Failing to understand how the mission of the nonprofit and the mission of the city in this example lead to emphasis or deemphasis on different activities can lead to unnecessary friction in the partnership.

In some rare cases, partners in a collaboration may have missions and values which seem to conflict. Collaboration may take place however if the various partners see something they can get out of the collaboration. It may be that they only need to agree on the set of activities covered under the collaboration and not on the wider vision of their separate organizations. As they say, "politics makes for strange bedfellows."

4. Understand the constituencies of the other members.

Each actor in an intergovernmental collaboration is responsible to a different set of constituencies. The nonprofit organization staff member may feel that their chief constituency is the Board of Directors of their agency and their clients. A state agency employee may feel that the governor, the legislature, and the public are their chief constituencies. And of course none of those constituencies may be singular. "The public" may translate to the members of the public who are active in interest groups who follow the issue on which you are collaborating. Similarly, there are many members of the Legislature and it is not surprising that they do not speak with one voice.

It is not only important that you understand your own constituency, it is also important that you understand what groups and forces are impacting the other actors in your intergovernmental collaboration. What may seem like needlessly resistant behavior on the part of one of your partners may be their attempt to represent the voices of some cross section of their constituents. The challenge is in allowing members of the collaboration to represent those differing views while still finding successful ways to work together.

5. Understand the particular statutes and rules that impact the other participants.

Some intergovernmental partners will be directly impacted by statutory language that requires certain activities or prevents others that impact your collaboration. It is not uncommon for state agency employees to know the particular Idaho code that sets up the parameters for their program. The same is true of federal employees. The same dynamics apply to administrative rules and regulations. Collaborations that seem to threaten compliance with these statutes and regulations will engender resistance from these state, local, and federal employees. To be an effective collaborator with agencies and governments that are directly impacted by statutes like this requires that the participants be given the chance to air their concerns and discuss the limitations and then evaluate what, if any, collaborative effort can happen within these constraints.

6. Understand the professional preparation and point of view of the other participants.

All of us are shaped by the education and professional preparation that we have experienced that bring us to this point and this collaboration. These different forms of preparation can shape our point of view on issues and processes.

For example, a scientist who has been trained in the field of biology will bring a set of assumptions about the value of science and the scientific method to questions of whether or not to introduce wolves into a particular ecosystem. A rancher, on the other hand, may be thinking mostly about the economics of his ranching operation when evaluating information about wolves. These two different points of view can lead to disagreement over what kinds of information to use in a collaborative process and how to value those various kinds of information. An effective collaborator will understand how our different professional backgrounds and approaches shape what kind of information we value and how we use information. One can easily see the challenges of combining accountants, members of the clergy, scientists, soldiers, and every other walk of life that leads us to where we are now.

7. Understand that it will take more time and resources to collaborate but that we can and must do so!

Sometimes the difficulties of intergovernmental collaboration make people wish they could just go back to their own cubicle and not worry about dealing with other agencies and units of government. Effective governance, however, requires that we figure out how to work together. In this time of diminished budgets and heightened expectations, we all owe our constituents and the public our best efforts at finding new ways to best meet our pressing needs. So we need collaboration even though it is harder than working alone. Providing yourself, your staff, and your boss with a realistic understanding of the additional time, resources and effort that collaboration requires is critical. There is an investment that has to be made in building and sustaining the collaboration. It may be tempting to try to avoid this investment in the hopes that the collaboration will save money later. A realistic understanding of the extra time and effort and resources that an effective collaboration requires will help each partner bring the necessary ingredients to the table to create and sustain the partnership.

Source: Witt (2010).

Spending time with the individuals in a collaborative effort is important to building trust. While a crisis may force agencies to communicate, more effective responses to an emergency will result if the responders are not making up the collaborative infrastructure and operational details while evacuating citizens who are covered in toxic goo from their homes. Building interpersonal relationships is time-consuming work, but there is no substitute for the familiarity that personal contact provides.

Good intentions, shared purpose, and the right expertise must be harnessed through clear communication, management of conflict, and leadership. Interagency efforts have an enhanced probability of success when participants listen to each other and have enough mutual understanding to be effective. (See tips in "Being an Effective Intergovernmental Collaborator" box on p. 83.)

Knowledge of the basic theory of group communication provides a foundation for understanding the technical competencies for managing meetings and using parliamentary procedures. Leaders and participants in groups must realize the importance of task and maintenance dimensions in group interaction.

Types of Group Activities

All groups have two dimensions that require attention if they are to have long-term success: task and maintenance. The *task* dimension encompasses all of the behaviors that move toward accomplishing specific work. New leaders sometimes overfocus on task, neglecting the *maintenance* dimension, which examines the socio-emotional aspects that bond individuals together. Conversely, leaders who are overly social may spend too little time on accomplishing required tasks.

Managers who pay attention to task requirements check that each team member has sufficient information and tools get the work done and monitor the flow of conversation about decision points or work elements. Maintenance-focused managers encourage team members, help relieve tension, and help others see their mutual connections. Maintenance work motivates individuals to cooperate toward the achievement of larger goals, as in the establishment of ground rules for group interaction. Individuals determine how they wish to interact with each other and what rules will govern how they deliberate as a group.

> **Tip:** Individuals who do not feel engaged in the process will have half-hearted commitment to group decisions.

Meeting Management

Holding meetings is one of the more vexing workplace activities—both for meeting managers and for those who attend. If meetings are

Table 6.2

Reasons to Hold a Meeting

- What is the goal for the meeting? Can the goal be articulated so those who attend understand the need?
- If the meeting is mostly informational, do the individuals need to meet face-to-face or can you just send out a memo?
- Is there a social or group-building reason to hold the meeting?
- Is there a statutory reason to hold the meeting?
- Is feedback or discussion of an issue needed or desired?
- Are there decisions the group should help make?

not perceived as salient to individual or group goals, those who attend may feel resentment toward meeting planners—and for good reason. Prevailing opinion among workers frequently is that meetings are a waste of time—and too often they are. To avoid these difficulties, leaders can follow the guidelines presented here before the meeting, during the meeting, and after the meeting. Effective leaders understand that meeting planning and management cannot be staffed out entirely to subordinates.

Before the Meeting

Eight steps should be taken as a part of premeeting management. First, analyze the purpose of the meeting to ensure it is necessary. In communications with those who will attend the meeting, articulate a specific purpose for the meeting to create a sense of importance for the occasion. Before scheduling a meeting, consider the questions in Table 6.2.

Second, give attendees sufficient notice. At times, due notice is a statutory or regulatory requirement, for example when a meeting is covered by an open meeting law. If meeting notification is discretionary, apply the criteria that everyone who needs or might desire to attend should have at least two reminders about when, where, and why the meeting will occur. For intra- or interagency meetings, an e-mail when a meeting is first scheduled and a one-day prior reminder should suffice. For public meetings, several channels of communication should be used so individuals feel the agency made a good faith effort to get their attention: press releases, website information, personal invitations to key stakeholder groups, or letters to those residing in affected geographic areas may be necessary.

Third, review the chairperson's notes from the previous meeting. Are there items to carry forward? Were there interpersonal issues that the leader should address between meeting sessions? For example, if one person seemed to dominate the discussion, will a chat with that person before the next meeting be effective in persuading him or her to moderate the level of participation? If someone acted inappropriately during the meeting (eye rolling while another was speaking), would a chat with that person prior to the next meeting about the behavior be appropriate? Were assignments given that need to be verified as completed before placing them on the agenda?

Some meeting chairs suffer from the impulse to talk too much. If the meeting purpose requires input, it is the chairperson's responsibility to create a space where discussion can occur. That responsibility extends to the chairperson's impulse to talk too much or to fill every pause. Sometimes a lingering pause allows those who are more reticent to enter the conversation. Conversely, the responsibility to manage a discussion may be betrayed by chairpersons who are too passive—allowing others to talk too much or stray from the agenda. When preparing for a meeting, consider what the chairperson must do to maintain control while allowing discussion among participants.

Fourth, prepare an agenda. Some meetings have statutory, bylaw, or other rules for agenda publication and guidelines for preparing an agenda. Review any laws, regulations, bylaws, or traditions that affect how the meeting will be structured.

Fifth, gather necessary resources to facilitate meeting success. In live meetings, check that projection equipment, whiteboards, and any other supplies are at hand. Prepare extra copies of the agenda or documents that participants may forget to bring to the meeting. For web meetings, ensure the proper equipment is present, working, and someone competent in its operation is available to handle breakdowns.

Sixth, confirm guest speaker attendance. Contact speakers or guests more than once, including a one-day advance reminder. Provide guests with directions and parking information. In secure facilities, prepare visitor badges and escorts through the building to the meeting room. While confirming the technical details, review with the guest his or her role during the meeting and how much time has been allotted.

Seventh, review skills to be used during the meeting. For contentious topics, plan strategies to maintain control without chilling discussion. Review parliamentary procedure rules for formal meetings.

Table 6.3

Common Mistakes by Meeting Chairpersons

1. Holding meetings that have no apparent purpose to attendees. A substantial number of meetings are convened for the wrong reasons.
2. Convening when the leader or key participants are unprepared.
3. Meeting without key participants or stakeholders. Are the right people in the room to provide information? Are the right people in the room to make decisions?
4. Having bad timing. Is the meeting scheduled when key participants are on vacation or off schedule? Is the meeting scheduled when employees will be taken away from critical agency operations? Should a meeting proceed if a critical incident has just occurred?
5. Doing too much talking. If the chairperson does most of the talking, the meeting should be relabeled as a briefing so participants do not expect opportunities to talk. Leaders who state an opinion and then ask for feedback chill participation from those who are not comfortable disagreeing with the boss.
6. Being so lax in structure that only some individuals do most of the talking or letting topics drift too far from the stated agenda without a justifiable reason.
7. Allowing the group to multitask, text message, and so forth, rather than attend to the discussion.
8. Allowing passive-aggressive misbehavior or incivility. Meeting chairs should set expectations for civil behavior.

Eighth, arrive early enough to manage any last-minute surprises and socialize with attendees. Premeeting socializing serves a maintenance function and helps participants feel more comfortable with each other.

During the Meeting

On the day of the meeting, the chairperson guides the group through several task and maintenance activities. First, start on time. A chairperson who starts late may unknowingly create a norm that meetings scheduled on the hour really start at a quarter past—so that is when the majority of attendees will arrive. Unless there are unusual reasons to do otherwise, start meetings within one or two minutes of the scheduled time.

Second, the chairperson should begin a meeting with orientation remarks to focus attention on the agenda and remind attendees of the goal for the meeting. If the chairperson cannot think of appropriate orientation remarks, perhaps the session is not needed.

Third, as the meeting progresses, balance social and task functions. Attendees will have varying expectations about what happens during an effective meeting. Some believe meetings are all work. Others think a

---

Skill Development
Strategic Brainstorming

Brainstorming can be used to keep the group from adopting the first reasonable idea, enhance participation from more individuals, spur creative
thinking, or interrupt conflict among contesting groups. The rules for
successful brainstorming are as follows:

1. State that the group will try brainstorming around a specific idea for
   five minutes (or some short amount of time).
2. State the rules for brainstorming

   - Everyone has to participate (either go around the room or have some
     other method of ensuring windbags do not dominate the exercise)
   - All ideas are welcome; even "crazy" ideas might spur ideas that
     become workable
   - No criticizing any of the ideas verbally or nonverbally; the next stage
     will analyze all of the ideas.

3. Record each idea onto large sticky pads or separate sheets of paper that
   can be displayed on a wall.
4. At the end of the brainstorming time, move into analysis by asking the
   group to gather around the ideas posted on the wall. Frame their next
   task as a question: "Let's see if any combination of items has potential
   for a solution that would be best for the agency, the public, and the
   group in the room."

---

meeting can be a fun social time. To balance these disparate expectations,
the chairperson encourages premeeting "chat" time to fulfill social needs
and then keeps the group relatively on-task during the business part of
the discussion. In less formal groups, the chair must balance letting the
conversation stray a bit off topic with allowing too much social talk. A
tool called the rubber band technique allows participants to stretch the
boundaries of a topic. The chairperson lets the discussion expand and
then brings the group back to the main item of discussion: "OK, we've
had some discussion about how other units might be affected by our new
rule—that's good to remember for future discussion. At this point, let's
focus back on the main decision we need to make today."

Fourth, provide everyone the opportunity to speak. The chairperson
may need to quiet those who overcontribute and encourage individuals
who undercontribute. There are many style and cultural reasons that affect

how much an individual will speak. Setting a norm that the chairperson expects everyone's input can change the discussion pattern. The chair can ask for everyone to contribute on a topic, go around the room in a systematic way to seek input, or use other techniques to elicit comments. Sometimes the chairperson will directly ask a person who can't seem to get into the conversation for his or her ideas. It is better to cue the individual that a chance to speak is coming rather than to put the person on the spot in an embarrassing way. "I've noticed that Stuart hasn't had a chance to add his comments yet into the discussion. I'm going to ask you in a minute for your thoughts. First, I want to remind everyone that we have another half hour for conversation on this topic and then we need to make a decision." By talking for a few seconds after cueing Stuart, time is given for him to think about what he wants to say.

Brainstorming is another technique that a meeting manager can use to expand participation and generate new ideas (see skill development box on strategic brainstorming for details).

Fifth, seek clarity. If individuals seem to misunderstand each other, use mysterious acronyms, or other confusion arises, it is the leader's job to ask questions and ensure all group members share the same understanding. Individual group members may not ask for clarification for fear of looking "stupid" in front of the boss. To mitigate this risk, the chairperson asks open-ended questions that clarify a point for everyone. "What do you mean when you say . . ." "I'm not sure what report you are referring to. Can you clarify?" "To be sure we all know what HMEP means, can you define that for us?" The fact that university libraries and agencies have help sites to translate the many thousands of acronyms in government underscores the need to seek clarity.

Sixth, summarize decisions. Regardless of which decision method is used (e.g., voting, consensus, chairperson decision), the meeting leader should repeat and confirm all decisions that are made using specific and unambiguous language. Likewise, any assignments made to staff should be summarized. These decisions are recorded in the meeting minutes.

Seventh, manage conflict. Discussion in meetings can be passionate, but it should not be uncivil. Chairpersons can acknowledge that individuals care deeply about the topic, while at the same time asking them to speak passionately for their goal without being disrespectful to others. Commonality statements may help the chairperson moderate incivility or conflict ("Even though we may differ on how to conduct the project, let's remember that we are all committed to the same end

---

Table 6.4

Managing Difficult Group Member Behaviors

- Ask the person to help you at the next meeting. ("I can see you have lots of ideas. Can you help me get some creativity going in the group by hanging back and making the third or fourth comment rather than the first?")
- Give the person a special job—recorder, timer, researcher for a new topic.
- Use a process that gives everyone a chance to speak.
- Work on ground rules for civil participation as a group, and then ask those who break the ground rules to rephrase their comments.
- Discuss the substantive issue in private before the meeting with someone who tends to over contribute.
- Privately ask others to help by directing their comments to those who have trouble getting into the conversation.

Source: Jones (2003).

---

goal"). Likewise, the chairperson can reframe inelegant statements into statements more suitable for discussion. "Your staff is incompetent" can be reframed as "Sounds like there's a work outcome that isn't everything you need. What specific work goal are you referring to?"

If the leader cannot manage the group conflict, he or she should utilize an outside facilitator who can control the group process and moderate dysfunctional behavior. Groups that manage member conflict are more effective than groups that do not (Kuhn and Poole 2000).

Eighth, manage time. The chairperson must be aware of the available time and move the discussion appropriately. In general, put announcements last or only in written form so these items do not consume the limited time available for group contributions.

Ninth, provide closure. At the end of the meeting, the chairperson must summarize what was accomplished; progress made, decisions achieved, training completed, and so forth. Any tasks assigned to specific individuals should be listed, as well as their deadlines. The time and place of the next meeting should be disclosed.

After the Meeting

As one meeting concludes, it is time to prepare for the next. Make notes of meeting management skills that worked well and those that might need improvement. Keep a list of assignments made and mark your calendar to follow up with each individual on his or her progress. Start the agenda for the next meeting with notes of any reports that will be due or issues that will carry forward. Mark your calendar to send the next agenda, perform tasks to prepare for the next meeting, including strategy preparation.

The Specialized Leadership Skill of Building Teams

What Is a Team?

Individuals at any level of an organization may be selected to lead a project. A group of individuals with the combined skills necessary to accomplish the task could be convened to work with a designated leader. Just because someone "convened" a task force does not make that individual a team leader or those who attend the meeting a team. A *team* is a relatively stable work group (for some length of time) in which the output is the collective effort of the group. Each team member is accountable to each other person. Casual groups or units where work is accomplished independently lack the critical defining element of mutual accountability that characterizes a team. Most work units are made up of individuals doing tasks proximate to each other rather than integrated with each other.

Teams are special. High-performance teams exhibit the following characteristics: (1) strategic leadership (clear mission, smart objectives, and realistic connection to the rest of the organizational environment); (2) process ownership (the team communicates well, has a creative climate, applies individual skills to the task as necessary, and measures its performance); (3) solid organization (have the right personnel, are results driven, have defined roles, communicate well, and members trust one another to perform); and (4) strategic team design (can-do culture, rewards given at the team level rather than at individual levels, and the organization invests in development of the team's technical and communicative prowess). (See Chiu, Lin, and Chien 2009; Klein et al. 2009; Pryor et al. 2009.)

Team building can be applied to many contexts. For example, a jurisdiction with conflict between the county council and the clerk's office staff might engage in team building focused on understanding each unit's roles and responsibilities and establishing guidelines for more effective communication. By understanding each other's roles and communication needs, the two groups can work together as a team (Giegold and Dunsing 1978).

Table 6.5

Questions to Ask Before Creating a Team

1. Are the work tasks interdependent (or should they be)?
2. Is the work short or long term?
3. Will the people ever work together again?
4. What is the nature of the relationship among the individuals?

Source: Funke (2012).

How Can We Create Teams?

The initial meeting of a team or task force is crucial to its success. In particular, is there an appropriate person in the team who has the disposition and communication skills to serve as its leader or is a professional facilitator needed? Some groups prosper with internal self-management and some require an objective outsider to facilitate their sessions. Some managers are prepared to lead teams and some are not.

Ideally the leader arranges for the group to meet in person to work on four key elements: purpose, roles and responsibilities, procedures, and team relationships (Kanaga and Prestridge 2004). Team members should be introduced to each other, understand the strategic importance of their task, and investigate who will have which responsibilities as they progress through the procedures necessary to accomplish the task. Sometimes the leader will prepare the procedures and responsibilities in advance and sometimes the team is engaged in that process.

For any project, understanding the importance of the task to the unit's overall mission is important. Being a team member tasked to work on an unfulfilling project that you don't believe is important will seem like a waste of time and energy. Likewise, a project lacking clear objectives, timelines, and output objectives may drag on too long. Depending on how it is perceived, being assigned to a team can be a reward that offers opportunities to learn new skills and meet others who might be helpful for career advancement, or being assigned to a team can be perceived as a punishment and distraction from one's primary job.

Whether a short-term team working on a project or a permanent team-based work group, establishment of norms for communication, processes, and treatment of each other is helpful. Research has dem-

---

Insights from the Field
Leading the New Task Force

A professor with proven facilitation skills was selected to lead a team of faculty and staff to investigate why retention of freshmen was so low at their university and to make recommendations for improvement. At the first meeting, each team member discussed personal areas of expertise and what skills, background, or organizational information he or she might bring to the overall task. Then the leader engaged the team in a structured discussion of what facts were needed to accomplish the task. After listing all their information needs, the leader then asked who at the university might know other facts or act as resources that would be useful to the group. The lists were then organized into three clusters for the information-gathering phase of the project: What other universities have experience with freshmen retention? What is already known about freshmen at this university? Who at the university already was involved in freshmen retention? The team members broke into three groups with firm deadlines for the initial investigation phase. In this case, asking the group about what should be investigated and how it should be organized energized the group, drew them together, and created a sense of ownership of the project.

---

onstrated that "bad apples" do bring down the performance of work teams if left unchecked. Felps, Mitchell, and Byington (2006) identify three common types of bad apples: those who dodge responsibilities and withhold effort (shirkers, free riders, and social loafers), those with negative moods, and those who violate interpersonal norms (use hurtful humor or sarcasm, inappropriate racial or sexual comments, cursing, pranking, rudeness, or conveyers of public embarrassment). When the bad apple cannot be ousted or ostracized, that person's presence produces feelings in others of inequity, negativity, defensiveness and reduced trust in the group, which in turn can lead to behavior changes that reduce productivity.

Leaders at all levels of public employment may have the opportunity to participate in teams. Recognizing that a team is more than a list of names is the first step in appropriate team creation and management.

Table 6.6

Typical Team Problems

1.	Floundering	Some teams start work on the task very slowly.
2.	Overbearing or dominating participants	Some members talk too much or work too hard to get have their ideas prevail.
3.	Withdrawing	Some members do not contribute ideas that would be helpful to the group effort.
4.	Unquestioning or attributing	Some groups do not test ideas and accept opinions or attributions as proven fact.
5.	Rushing to accomplishment	Some groups do not spend enough time on problem analysis.
6.	Discounting	Some groups discount or ignore potentially good ideas rather than treating all ideas and contributions with respect.
7.	Wandering	Some groups lose focus and move off task.
8.	Feuding	People cannot overcome personal or philosophical differences and consume the group's time with discord.

Source: Adapted from Van Wart (2011).

Parliamentary Procedure

Many boards, commissions, nonprofit assemblies, and other organizations use Robert's Rules of Order as their organizing structure. Whenever formal guidelines constrain how a group operates, leaders and participants should have a working knowledge of the rules. When written rules are present, inadvertently breaking the rules may make decisions unenforceable. If a leader is not aware of proper rule structure, meeting participants can delay or divert the operations of governance by manipulating the rules.

The Basic Rules of Order

The philosophy upholding most rule systems seeks stability and fairness by keeping order in a consistent way. Robert's Rules were developed as an antidote to chaos. If anyone could speak about anything as long as he or she wished, efficiency and equity would suffer. Robert's Rules provide a stately process for making decisions in the midst of dissention.

Rules protect those in the majority and those in the minority. Sadly,

Table 6.7

The Standard Agenda in Parliamentary Procedure

Call to order (establish a quorum)
Reading and approval of the minutes
Officer reports
Committee reports
Unfinished business
New business
Announcements
Adjournment

rules also can be manipulated in ways that hamstring the processes of government (as several sessions of Congress have illustrated). Ideally, rules protect the majority by providing ways to stop those in the minority from delaying a decision (for example, motions to end debate or to limit the amount of time any one speaker can have the floor). Those in the minority opinion have the right to speak on an issue and to use tactics that encourage the search for compromise (for example, motions to table, reconsider, or send to committee). All individuals are ensured the right to speak when recognized by the chair, to introduce motions, and to vote on issues before the group.

The tables in this chapter present a parliamentary procedure primer for beginners. If you participate in organizations that use Robert's Rules or another rule book, bring the rules and bylaws with you to each meeting. If you conduct meetings using a rule book, become knowledgeable of typical motions or secure the services of a parliamentarian to attend meetings and advise you on sticky points of procedure. At large board of director meetings, the person sitting nearest the presiding officer often is a parliamentarian who unobtrusively coaches the chair on how to respond to various motions raised by delegates.

Table 6.7 illustrates the standard agenda for most meetings. Each element should be taken in order. Specific details about how each item is acted upon may be present in the organization's bylaws. For example, the bylaws will state that a quorum (the number of people present before business can be conducted) is a set percentage of voting members. Robert's Rules of Order illustrates the formal language used to introduce each type of business.

Unless there were leftover items from the last meeting or items postponed to the current one, most business will occur within the new business section. While there are many exotic motions, the most frequently

Table 6.8

Common Motions

Motion	Member Says	Chairperson Says	Second Req.	Debatable	Amendable	Vote Level
Main	"I move that . . ."	"It has been moved and seconded that. . . Is there any discussion?"	YES	YES	YES	Majority
To Amend	"I move to amend the motion by . . ."	"It has been moved and seconded to amend the motion by . . . Is there any discussion?"	YES	YES	YES	Majority
Move Question	"I move the previous question."	"It has been moved and seconded that we close debate on the issue before us. Those in favor? . . . Those opposed?" The motion to close debate passes/fails."	YES	NO	NO	2/3[a]
Lay on the Table	"I move to table the motion."	"It has been moved and seconded to table the motion. All in favor . . . All opposed . . . The motion to table passes/fails."	YES	NO	NO	Majority[b]
Refer to Committee	"I move to refer the motion to the _____ committee."	"It has been moved and seconded to refer the motion to the _____ committee. Is there any discussion?"	YES	YES	YES	Majority
To adjourn	"I move to adjourn."	"It has been moved and seconded that we adjourn. All in favor? . . . Opposed? The motion to adjourn passes/fails."	YES	NO	NO	Majority

Notes: Consult the specific rules of the group to ensure these general guidelines apply.

a. The vote is too close debate on an amendment or main motion. If the "motion on the previous question" passes, then a vote is immediately taken on the question at hand.

b. If a motion or amendment is tabled, all subsidiary motions also are tabled as a package and cannot come back to consideration until a motion to take from the table passes (which can occur on the same day).

used will be main motions, amendments, motions to reconsider, and motions to take from the table. It is useful to have a schematic chart of the precedence of which type of motion will be considered first. These charts are available in virtually any published version of Robert's Rules of Order and at http://www.constitution.org/rror/rror-01.htm.

Motions are formal statements that request action by the group (see Table 6.8). While business begins with a main motion ("I move that we buy eight new police cars"), main motions have the least power in the order of precedence. Many things can happen to main motions before they reach a vote: amendments, replacement, tabling, sending to committee, and so forth.

Amendments substantively change the details of a main motion ("I move to amend the main motion to buy six new police cars"). Substitute motions replace the original main motion with something else ("I move a substitute motion that we trade our ten old police cruisers for four new motorcycle units"). Amendments and substitute motions can, in turn, be amended.

A motion to reconsider asks the participants to put a motion that was completed previously (i.e., voted on) back on the table for consideration. To keep malcontents from using this motion as a means of slowing business, only someone who voted in the majority on a main motion can make a motion to reconsider. This explains why a member who is in the opposition may sometimes vote for a measure they don't agree with— he or she is hoping new information will allow a successful motion to reconsider at a later date.

Tabling a motion is an appropriate way to delay action until more information is acquired, and often is used to kill a motion ("I move we table the motion to buy new police cruisers"). When a motion is tabled, it is taken from the agenda and can only return when a successful motion to take the item from the table passes ("I move we take the proposal to buy a police cruiser from the table").

Different motions may or may not require a second, may or may not be debatable, and require various percentages of favorable votes to pass. Table 6.8 provides a sampling of the requirements for common motions.

Mayhem and Miscues in the Parliamentary World

Common miscues in the use of parliamentary procedure may be cause for amusement or havoc, depending on the people involved and the context.

Table 6.9

Parliamentary Miscues

- Chair asks if there are any corrections to the minutes and then ask for a vote to approve or amend—*no vote is required.*
- Officer and committee reports are offered for a vote of approval—*no motions or vote are required.*
- Chair acting on motions without seconds when seconds are required or asking for a second when it is not required.
- Members introducing a motion by saying "I motion that . . ." rather than "I move that . . ."
- Chair hears the motion to *ask(call) for the question* ("I move the previous question") and proceeds immediately to a vote on the issue. Moving the previous question really is a motion asking for a vote to close debate, not to vote immediately on the issue.
- Chair accepts more than two main motions on the table at the same time. Only one main motion can be on the table at a time.

In less formal meetings, mistakes typically are benevolently ignored. In contexts where meetings are recorded or small errors may be grounds for legal action, greater attention to detail is necessary. Some common miscues are listed in Table 6.9.

Case: The Interdepartment Team

The governor has issued Executive Order 2013–25, which authorizes the creation of a special bicentennial celebration for your state's upcoming anniversary. A task force composed of workers from across state government will have primary responsibility for the organization of the yearlong series of events. As deputy director of the state historical society, you have been given the task of organizing this team. When you meet with your boss, the director of the historical society, she hands you a list of the task force members and tells you, "I know you'll have a great team."

Discussion Question

1. What are the key steps you will need to take to ensure the creation of an effective team to organize the state's bicentennial celebration?

7

Dealing with Incivility, Bullies, and Difficult People

> *In a defensive routine, no one is*
> *thinking that win-win is an option.*
> —William Noonan, in *Discussing the Undiscussable*

Ideally, the workplace is a comfortable environment, free from inter-personal stress and bad behavior. Too often, the workplace is a site for incivility, bullying, and encounters with troublesome behaviors from coworkers, bosses, clients, or the public. Incivility, bullying, workplace aggression, and illegal harassment are aggregated under the general title of workplace misbehavior. Vardi and Weitz (2004) conclude: "Our review of the literature suggests that misbehavior in organizations should not only be viewed as *pervasive*, but for the most part, as *intentional* work-related behavior mostly (yet not necessarily) bearing *negative consequences* for both individuals (perpetrators and targets) and the organization" (p. 28). Because illegal workplace behaviors such as sexual harassment and maltreatment of protected classes receive quality treatment in numerous other sources, this chapter focuses on forms of harassment and antisocial behaviors that currently are not covered under most state, provincial, and federal laws.

Verbal Aggression and Difficult People

Workplace aggression has been classified as either verbal or physical, passive or active, and direct or indirect (Baron and Neuman 1996, 1998). Workplace aggression is more often verbal than physical (Coombs and Holladay 2004), putting it firmly in the sphere of communication. "Most workplace aggression is enacted through communication, communication is a mechanism for responding to workplace aggression, and it is a primary means for delivering policies designed to eliminate workplace aggression" (Coombs and Holladay 2004, p. 482).

One of the most common dysfunctional work behaviors is verbal aggression. This includes both direct and indirect verbal actions, such as ridicule, character attacks, questioning others' competence, making fun of someone's physical appearance, hurtful teasing, insults, spreading rumors, yelling, or intentional patterns of interruptions. Nonverbal aggression or passive-aggressive tactics may include dirty looks, aggressive or obscene gestures, hiding needed resources, sabotage of someone's workplace, being intentionally late to meetings, delaying work to make others look bad, malicious mischief-making, failure to return messages, refusing to talk to someone, or failure to warn management of potential problems (Coombs and Holladay 2004; Kassing and Avtgis 1999; Keashly and Jagatic 2003; Vardi and Weitz 2004). Verbal aggressiveness is different from argumentativeness. The latter characterizes people who enjoy verbal sparring and testing ideas through good-natured debate. Argumentativeness may be valuable or annoying in a work setting, but is not, in itself, a type of workplace misbehavior. Verbal aggressiveness, on the other hand, sets the aggressor in a one-up position over the other person, often precipitating a defensive reaction that leads to a cycle of recrimination and escalation.

While some organizations consider workplace aggression acceptable if productivity or serving the public is not adversely affected, there are significant reasons why organizations should care about problematic workplace behaviors. Madlock and Dillow (2012) found supervisor verbal aggression was directly related to worker dissatisfaction. Other research indicates that attention to workplace aggression is particularly important during times of work stress, job insecurity, cost cutting, or organizational change (Baron and Neuman 1998). When workplace misbehavior affects employees or accomplishment of the agency's mission, it is the responsibility of supervisors and upper administrators to take notice and to respond appropriately.

Appropriate response by supervisors is important. As discussed in Chapter 5, too much intrusiveness for the wrong reasons can demotivate employees. Yet, inattentive management can be even more deleterious. When faced with problematic behavior, supervisors should conduct an analysis of the situation. For example, the techniques discussed in this book apply only to midrange behaviors—behaviors influenced by alcohol, drugs, some psychological dysfunctions, or violence are beyond the average supervisor's scope of knowledge. In particular, if violence is present, threatened, or implied, one should extract oneself from the immediate situation and consult human resource or law enforcement professionals.

If it seems appropriate for a supervisor to proceed to a response, analysis should include consideration of the multitude of causes for problematic behaviors:

1. Coworkers or the supervisor could in some way be provoking the observed verbal aggressiveness or workplace misbehavior.
2. The observed behavior could be a workplace manifestation of difficulties an employee is facing at home or other nonwork aspects of his or her life.
3. The workplace misbehavior might be a habitual pattern in the employee.
4. There might be a misunderstanding of intention due to the employee's poor communication skills.
5. If the employee displaying the apparent misbehavior is from a different culture than other employees or the supervisor, cross-cultural issues may be manifesting.

The general cause of a specific situation will change the supervisor's response choices, which can focus on behavior or on policy. Regardless of the cause, supervisors and managers have a role to play in transforming problematic employee behavior into more productive activities.

Problematic behaviors from members of the public can profit from similar causal analysis. Sometimes fear impels aggressive communication. Understanding citizens' fears can help in shaping messages to work on issues without precipitating fearful reactions.

One of the dynamics that deters appropriate responses to problematic behavior in others is a feeling of indignation about a situation. Sims (2005) explains that indignation negates feeling of responsibility for any part of the situation and generates an enhanced judgment of personal "rightness" (i.e., it is the other person's problem). Those who feel indignation seem more open to demonizing and negatively labeling the other person. Regardless of the "rightness" of the situation, feelings of moral superiority may further deteriorate the work climate and create a secondary conflict about who is right. If not managed effectively, the emotional state of the coworker or supervisor may create new dimensions of the problem and make the situation worse.

Two important insights come from this discussion about thought-

---

Insights from the Field
Common Workplace Misbehavior

A Utah Human Resources Officer

The most common violation of our code of ethics policy is disrespectfulness to coworkers or other employees in the workplace—being unprofessional and engaging in an unprofessional way or just failing to get along in the workplace. I think people don't understand that you have to be professional at work, and you don't have to like each other, but you have to work together.

I frequently have situations where there are employees who are not very respectful to their supervisors, and that would be in their tone of voice or hanging up the phone when the supervisor is speaking with them. Sometimes an employee doesn't like another employee and they avoid them in the workplace and things become uncomfortable. We once had an employee that spat on another employee. But our code of ethics policy is very detailed, and talks about ethics with clients and the public, client records, communications with the clients and the public, and in work relationships. So employees are required to treat each other respectfully and professionally, use nonabusive, polite, and decent language. This prohibits any activity that is demeaning, belittling, or offensive. Respect the religious values and cultural differences of colleagues. Avoid slanderous or malicious gossip. Gossip is another problem in the workplace.

---

fully analyzing problematic behaviors. First, everyone in the workplace affects workplace climate; everyone's communication can be a part of the problem or a part of the solution. Second, unless problem behavior is caused by a psychological condition requiring treatment, future behavior often is more important than the original cause of the behavior. This leads to an important question for public managers: How should I respond to misbehavior?

Skills to Respond to Workplace Misbehavior

Workers who are effective and experience less stress from interactions with colleagues and the public have a wide array of communication skills in their list of competencies. This section presents several options for responding to problematic workplace behavior.

Responding to Control Issues

Some behaviors that are evaluative, sarcastic, or just overly demanding for things to be "done my way" arise from an employee's basic need for control. In general, experts advise analysis of the controller's underlying interest and trying to manage the behavior at the interest level. If an employee is fearful of not being able to keep up with change, he or she may tightly control what they do understand. Attention to training and a progressive plan to acquire more team-based behavior might help. If someone intrudes beyond their responsibility into the supervisor's duties or another employee's job, clarifying boundaries and job responsibilities may help. Sometimes, creating a new task where the employee's energy is refocused will suffice to moderate misbehavior. When one employee thinks he or she knows the only "right" way to do a job or is a perfectionist, discuss the underlying "interest" in serving the public or the department's goal. Facilitating a discussion with the work unit can locate a common understanding of processes or lead to group decisions on how tasks should be accomplished. If the controlling behavior continues, the supervisor can then counsel the employee to see how the problematic behavior affects overall team goal achievement and establish an employee improvement plan.

Replying to Issues of Respect

> *I don't think it's ever OK to yell at your employees and call*
> *them stupid. They may have a lack of understanding about*
> *how they should be doing their job and let's address that.*
> *It's not a civil workplace if you're yelling.*
> —A Nevada State Government Human Resources Officer

The workplace in some ways is just another location where the usual range of misunderstanding and differences occur. Humans misunderstand each other's intentions on a regular basis. Small differences in habit can seem disrespectful. For example, if one employee enjoys greeting everyone in the morning with social talk (to make personal connections) and another silently walks around the chatting group to reach his desk (to get right to work), the avoidance of communication could be interpreted as aloofness or disrespect.

A common complaint against coworkers and supervisors is: "I don't get any respect." Respect is an ambiguous and personally idiosyncratic phenomenon. Even those intending to give respect can be perceived as being disrespectful.

Several tools are available to foster common viewpoints of respectful workplace behavior. Many agencies will have statements of common value, respectful workplace policies, or other declarations of what is and is not acceptable communication. Units can be engaged to develop statements of what it means to be respectful. Once developed, it is the supervisor's duty to ensure the ideas gain traction in the unit rather than become faded words on a forgotten poster in the employee break room. By modeling respectful communication and demanding it from others, supervisors can moderate dysfunctional workplace behaviors.

Managing the High-Conflict Individual

Some employees can be characterized as high-conflict. These individuals behave defensively, blame others, or engage in annoying approval-seeking behaviors (Eddy 2011). Depending on the type of high-conflict behavior, sometimes giving more attention can minimize the behavior. Instead of the employee behaving badly to get attention from the supervisor, the supervisor can briefly acknowledge the employee on a regular basis.

For those who habitually are defensive, negative, or excel in rumor mongering, lectures addressing their attitudes are rarely effective. Supervisors can respond with a variety of tactics, including the following:

1. Reframing negative comments into positive frames for discussion
2. Asking the individual to repeat comments without negative labeling of other individuals
3. Giving information to reduce their possible fear in situations rife with uncertainty
4. Setting boundaries of acceptable communication behaviors

Table 7.1 presents additional problematic workplace behaviors and suggested responses.

Bullying

Defining Bullying

While definitions vary, in the United States and Canada bullying is a type of harassment characterized by long-term (weeks or months), hurtful and intentional physical or verbal actions by one individual toward another

Table 7.1

Responses to Problematic Workplace Behaviors

Behavior	Response
Anger (excludes anger expressed in ways that you feel are dangerous or may be violent)	1. Assume anger comes from fear or an attempt to get your attention. 2. Avoid defensive responses. 3. Use emotional defusing listening techniques (see Chapter 3). 4. Reframe angry comments into work-related issues. 5. Refer the individual to counseling. 6. Use mapping technique to identify possible fears and respond at the fear/need level.
Personal self-interest	1. Reframe as larger work issues.
Interrupts when you are giving feedback	1. Listen, then return to your planned discussion rather than be drawn off-topic.
Argumentativeness	1. Ask for ideas and help in solving the problem instead of critique. 2. Assign the individual tasks requiring analytical ability. 3. Use the "Yes . . . and" technique.
Negativity or sarcasm	1. Ignore the negative comments and go on. 2. Reframe the comments. 3. Refer to department statements of common value or respectful workplace. 4. Coach the individual on how to restate the comment more productively.

individual in a lesser power position (see Leck and Galperin 2006). Bullying may occur between persons in seemingly equal organizational positions or even manifest as a subordinate bullying a weak supervisor (called bullying up). Randall (1997) claims that one difference between general verbal aggressiveness and bullying is intention: that is, anyone can have a bad day and strike out verbally but bullies behave badly toward targeted individuals repeatedly over time.

Sexual harassment or harassment of legally protected classes may fit the bullying definition and be designated as illegal. Table 7.2 explores some of the legal definitions that may apply to members of protected classes who are targets of bullying. For those outside of protected classes, the legal system either has not addressed routine workplace aggression and bullying or statues have such strict thresholds that even the most egregious cases have difficulty when litigated (Bible 2012). Lack of

Table 7.2

Bullying Compared to Illegal Discrimination and Harassment

Protected Class	Protected class is a term used in antidiscrimination law to describe individuals who cannot be targeted for discrimination or harassment. For example, typical laws identify groups of individuals that cannot be discriminated against based on characteristics including: race, color, religion, gender, age, sexual orientation, national origin, physical or mental disability, veteran status, genetic information, or any other status protected under applicable federal, state, or local law.
Illegal Discrimination	Discrimination occurs when an individual or group of individuals is treated adversely (i.e., denied rights, benefits, equitable treatment, or access to facilities available to all others) based on the individual's or group's protected class.
Harassment	Harassment is a form of discrimination. Harassment consists of unwelcome behavior that is based upon a person's protected class.
Bullying	Harassment of individuals who may or may not be included in a protected class.

specific legislation, however, does not mean that employers are not responsible for a bully's effects on coworkers.

Bully Behaviors

The behaviors of bullies are varied and widespread (see Lutgen-Sandvik and Tracy 2011). Bully behaviors share the characteristic of being an intentional and relentless campaign against a targeted individual. The Generalized Workplace Harassment Questionnaire measures five bully-type behaviors: (1) verbal aggressiveness such as yelling, verbal disrespect, or hostile exchanges; (2) disrespectful behavior such as demeaning language or public humiliation; (3) isolation such as having work efforts compartmentalized or ignored; (4) threats and bribes to commit or ignore wrong things; and (5) physical aggression (Shannon, Rospenda, and Richman 2007).

Table 7.3 presents Lutgen-Sandvik's (2003) cycle of bully behavior. Since bullying occurs over time, it may follow a pattern of gradually increasing intensity that occurs in several stages. Stage 1 bulling is amenable to tactics a target can use with a bully. After Stage 2, the bully has manipulated the situation sufficiently that targets need help from others.

Table 7.3

Cycle of Workplace Emotional Abuse

Stage 1:   Initial incident of bullying or verbal abuse (sometimes related to staff changes or organization changes)—cycle begins when the abuse continues after the initial incident.

Stage 2:   Progressive discipline—the victim's work suffers or the bully's negative comments persuade a supervisor to discipline the victim.

Stage 3:   Turning point—the bully successfully brands the victim as the problem; target unsuccessfully attempts to get help from the supervisor or coworkers.

Stage 4:   Organizational ambivalence—upper management becomes aware of the problem and usually spots the victim as the problem.

Stage 5:   Isolation—coworkers withdraw support from the victim.

Stage 6:   Expulsion—the victim is fired or quits. A new employee arrives and becomes the next potential victim.

Source: Lutgen-Sandvik (2003).

Extent and Effects of Bullying

It is difficult to determine the amount of bullying that occurs in the public sector—partly because researchers use different measurement tools and partly because most studies focus on the private sector (Keashly and Jagatic 2003). A U.S. study by the Workplace Bullying and Trauma Institute (Namie 2003) included government workers and found 61 percent of respondents were being bullied at the time of the study. A 2006 general workplace bulling study estimated around 10 percent of the total workforce is experiencing bullying at any one time (Tracy, Lutgen-Sandvik, and Alberts 2006).

An Australian study found 33 percent of public sector workers had been bullied in their current workplace with the adverse behaviors occurring both in private and public settings. Forty-seven percent of victims did not lodge complaints against the bully (Omari 2007). Randall estimated that workplace aggression and bullying "caused some 500,000 employees to miss 1.7 million days of work annually" (1997, p. 48).

The amount of bullying estimated seems to vary widely depending on the country, employment sector, and study methodology. What does not vary is the effect. For those bullied over a long period of time, there was a 70 percent chance that the victim would lose his or her job. Namie

(2003) summarized: "Bullying is done with impunity. Perpetrators face a low risk of being held accountable. Targeted individuals pay by losing their once-cherished positions" (p. 3). The stress-related mental health effects of bullying are well documented (Nielsen and Einarsen 2012). Sperry and Duffy (2009) summarize the general impact of bullying:

> Because of the protracted time periods involved in most [bullying] epi-sodes, the [bullying] victim is worn down at a time when fear and uncer-tainty about the future is greatest. [Bullying] victims develop fear, anxiety, and concern about their employment future within the organization where the [bullying] occurred or their reemployability should they be fired or leave. Concerns about finances, health insurance, loss of professional and personal status, damage to reputation, self-doubt, loss of self-confidence, social isolation, and damage to psychological and physical health are addi-tional real and pressing sources of worry. The result, in terms of individual psychological trauma, is systemic overload, resulting in numbness, lack of ability to concentrate, and withdrawal. (pp. 434–435)

Like most social phenomenon, the monetary cost of bullying is dif-ficult to assess. One analyst estimated bullying cost Canadian for-profit companies $20,000 per employee per year (Reinhardt 2004). Organi-zational costs can be considerable, particularly when redress is sought through civil lawsuits. A review of public sector litigated cases involving bulling found "current legal protections seem to be somewhat limited in their efficacy in protecting victims of workplace bullying" and that civil lawsuits seemed more successful (LaVan, Katz, and Jedel 2010, p. 741). The presence of unions may or may not deter bullying or help in remedying the behavior. Management teams who tolerate bullying are wise to remember that "while currently there are no specific laws prohibiting workplace bullying, there are numerous tangential laws that could be used as the basis for litigation" (LaVan et al. 2010, p. 749; see also Sanders, Pattison, and Bible 2012).

Glendinning (2001) identified collateral effects in organizations that permit bullying such as getting a reputation as a bad place to work, stifling of creativity among workers, and fearful climates that chill personnel development and succession planning. In addition to litigation, bullying in the workplace can lead to increased staff turnover. The cost of hiring and retraining new employees can prove to be substantial. The negative impact on employee retention may expand beyond the targeted victim of bullying and result in higher turnover, driving up recruitment and training costs. Bartlett and Bartlett (2011) detail how absenteeism, loss of time, loss of creative effort, and other organizational effects of bullying relate to increased health care costs, a tougher recruiting climate, and increased worker compensation claims.

One concern about bullying in the workplace is that verbal aggressive behaviors that target employees may be a precursor to the bully (or victim) transitioning to physical violence. The literature is replete with examples of targets of workplace bullying shooting their coworkers or bosses (Baron and Neuman 1996).

Responding to the Bully

While we might think everyone should know how to behave at work or with the public, experience shows that not every employee has the same view of appropriate behavior. Responding to bullying, and all forms of inappropriate workplace behavior, must start with clear policy about what appropriate workplace behavior is and is not, as well as monitoring of behavior (with supervisor intervention and plans for improvement as necessary). As Glendinning states (2001), "your best bet to prevent future bullies is to catch them in their larval state" (p. 282).

Recent research has focused on how targets of bullying perceive and talk about the perpetrator's behaviors. Lutgen-Sandvik and McDermott (2011) claim that "how organizational members talk about and make sense of adult bullying, particularly the attributed causes, creates the social reality to which they respond" (p. 344). In other words, how a group talks about what happened and how the event is labeled determine responses. Lutzen-Sandvik and McDermott found several themes of sense-making about bullying that focused on different parts of the experience (the perpetrator's motives, how the organization's response was perceived, the victim's nature, and so forth). Each explanatory theme was nuanced in how it was talked about in the organization. For example, some perpetrators were described as evil, others as intentionally malicious, and some as power hungry. The significance of the research on how bullying is characterized is in the probable response—someone who is perceived as evil might be reacted to differently than someone who is seen as socially inept. The 50 percent of targets who characterized bullying as somehow their own fault already start from a position of weakness. Many of the perceptions about bullying create a sense of powerlessness in targets and work units (Lutgen-Sandvik and Tracy 2011).

Supervisors need the training, support, and tools to intervene and redirect dysfunctional employee behaviors and to label problematic behaviors appropriately. Behavior changes are best made early in the process before patterns become established and bullies feel their behavior tacitly is endorsed. Habit becomes the accepted pattern, which then becomes part of the unit's culture. While there is no "science" to explain why bullies develop in one organization and not in another, some similar characteristics seem to form a pattern that permits bullying: (1) deficiencies in supervision, (2) deficiencies in leadership, (3) availability of vulnerable victims, and (4) low morale (Harvey et al. 2009).

The Organization's Response

Lacking federal or state laws that regulate bullying (other than rules covering protected classes), organizations are on their own in deciding how to respond. Regardless of its causes, supervisors and directors should constrain this workplace malaise. Agencies can assess if they have the right tools to respond to workplace bullying by examining their rules and policies: Are standards for behavior clear and procedures in place to correct unwanted workplace behavior? Policy analysis is important. Cowan (2011) interviewed human resource (HR) officers in the private sector and discovered that many cited policies they believed would cover bullying when an analysis of the policy discovered it only covered protected classes. Other HR officers were uncertain if their workplace behavior policies included bullying or contained a means for employees to report such behavior. Only some HR personnel were cognizant that the bully's behavior can be very subtle or unobserved by others, thus making it difficult to prove (Cowan 2012).

If policies are not clear or do not include bullying, then several steps are warranted, as noted by Harvey et al. (2009):

1. Develop a standard operating rule and norm that bullying and harassing behaviors in the workplace are not tolerated.
2. Establish who is responsible for determining if behavior complies with policies/expectations.
3. Provide a procedure for supervisors and department heads to use when bullying emerges.
4. Link the new procedure to other grievance or personnel processes.
5. Identify penalties and due process procedures.

In state or federal agencies, any new policy should be vetted to ensure fidelity with existing policies, state or federal laws, and union contracts. Formal rules and processes provide standards and a lever to change behavior. Modern practices, however, suggest supervisors also need tools to coach employees in changing problematic behavior rather than just filling out forms for punitive action against an employee.

As policies or standards for workplace behavior are developed, employees should be included as much as possible. Those who are engaged in creating polices are more committed to them. At minimum, inform employees of behavioral expectations, provide training on how to respond to problematic coworker behavior, train supervisors and department heads on how to explain the changes to employees, train supervisors and department heads on how to integrate the new behavioral expectations in periodic review criteria, and provide a coaching "safety net" for supervisors to increase the probability that they will follow through in helping employees meet the new standards.

Another tactic the organization can use to prevent bullying starts during the job interview process. Add language to job descriptions that employees are responsible for their interpersonal behavior and should treat all employees and the public with dignity and respect (Glendinning 2001). Nonprofits should prepare analogous standards and procedures for volunteers.

The Bystander's Response

Compounding strategies for responding to bullying are research findings suggesting that coworkers rarely help the victims of bullying. Bystanders may assume that management is controlling adverse behaviors or believe silence from supervisors is tacit encouragement for bullying. Likewise, victims often think that management would not support them, retaliation would occur if they reported the bully, and nothing would improve (Leck and Galperin 2006).

Adding to a bystander's dilemma is doubt about the bully's political or social connections. Leck and Galperin explain: "Even when anti-bullying practices are adopted, organizations may be reluctant to enforce them, especially if the bully is an otherwise effective and productive employee. Further, since bullies who "'get the job done' are often rewarded by promotion, they frequently occupy positions of power and are inherently 'fireproof'" (2006, p. 95).

The Target's Response

Bullying is a special type of workplace conflict. Because of its gradual escalatory nature and the inherent reduction of the victim's power, mid- to late-stage bullying typically cannot be managed with the conflict management skills that might be applicable in other difficult situations. Research finds that targets who were successful in responding to a bully took the following steps:

1. Set boundaries early or got out of the situation.
2. Sought help and longer-term leaves of absence to recover.
3. Had help from upper management such as firing the bully or moving the victim to another unit.

Zapf and Gross (2001) summarized: "nobody was able to achieve [recovery] without external help" (p. 505). The role of management in controlling bullying is essential. The most common strategy used by victims of bullying was conflict avoidance or other passive strategies—in other words, strategies that rarely succeed in reducing conflict (Zapf and Gross 2001). In other cases, conflict management attempts may be threatening to a bully and trigger the onset of the bully-target cycle. The best solutions involve active supervisor work to control workplace behaviors.

Many sources give suggestions for targets of bullying (Leck and Galperin 2006; Shannon, Rospenda, and Richman 2007, Tracy, Alberts, and Rivera 2007). Some common advice appears in Table 7.4. Communicative responses directed to the bully are the most effective during early stages of bullying. In later stages after the target has been stigmatized by the bully, strategic responses shift to seeking management help, having specific examples of the behavior documented to persuade management that the problem exists, and (sometimes) gathering data for formal grievances and lawsuits.

Case: Is The Behavior Problematic?

Situation 1

You are a new supervisor in a state unit with fifteen employees. Some are new employees and many have been with the agency for more than twenty years. During your first week, you observe a senior employee who

Table 7.4

Ways Targets Can Respond to Workplace Bullies

	Response
	1. Break the silence. State your personal feelings about the other's behavior (MacIntosh 2006; Randall 1997).
	2. Use *I statements*. "I feel embarrassed when you berate me in front of other employees." Be prepared for the "That's just the way I am and you need to deal with it" response.
	3. Try not to respond with sarcasm, labeling, or overgeneralizations; "You always . . ." or "He's such an egotistical jerk."
	4. Use the *broken record technique* and repeat your comments even if interrupted (Randall 1997).
Early Stages	5. Tell co-workers immediately; solicit help from co-workers before an adverse pattern is established or the bully has time to taint your image (MacIntosh 2006).
	6. Provide alternative behavior; "Instead of calling me stupid new guy, please call me new guy Henry."
	7. Contact your supervisor and human resources department for coaching assistance and to alert them to the workplace issue.
	8. Even when pressured and belittled, don't agree to anything or sign anything you do not agree with (Field 1996).
	9. Keep a journal. Keep copies of phone messages or record conversations (if legal); print abusive e-mails. Keep all records off the workplace location. Document all incidents, including how the incident made you feel (Field 1996; Kohut 2008; MacIntosh 2006).
Middle Stages	1. Go up the chain of command with your complaint; usually notify your direct supervisor that you are doing so.
	2. Be relevant and rational in the narrative told to management; describe what happened rather than call the bully names (Tracy, Alberts, and Rivera 2007).
	3. Have a back-up exit plan if management does not support your position. Conduct a cost-benefit analysis on whether to stay with the agency, litigate, or leave (Kohut 2008).
	4. Maintain emotional detachment; seek counseling; talk to trusted friends (Field 1996; Kohut 2008).
	5. Remind the organization or union of the potential costs if bullying continues: the bully could escalate to violence, decreased productivity from turnover, lawsuits, lack of ability to meet the agency's mission (Dierickx 2004).

is mentoring one of the new employees calling the newcomer "stupid" and giving scathing feedback where other employees can hear. The other employees leave the area (if they can) while the dressing down is occurring. From the perspective of the new supervisor, is there a problem?

Situation 2

You are a long-time manager in a nonprofit agency. A new supervisor was recently hired to oversee other employees in the agency's store where donated items are sold. You observe the new supervisor standing unusually close to an employee while berating him about a minor mistake. The employee is very shy, but you know he always received good evaluations from the previous supervisor. From the perspective of the long-term manager, is there a problem?

Situation 3

You are a new manager in a state agency. An employee comes to you and complains that her supervisor is a bully and treats her unfairly. You know that the supervisor's previously glowing evaluations of this employee turned negative about six months ago. When you ask for examples, the employee becomes flustered and says that the supervisor doesn't give her full instructions on how to do tasks and then evaluates her poorly and ignores her when she asks questions about the task. When you ask for another example, she says the supervisor rolls her eyes, makes a face, and ignores or cuts down any comments she makes during staff meetings. From the perspective of the new manager, is there a problem?

Case: There's Something About Jeremy

When Bob became supervisor of the internal audit division of the state Department of Administration he looked forward to meeting his new employees and getting to know them. At the first staff meeting, Bob was pleased to see the cheerful interaction among most of the staff. Not everyone, however, seemed happy.

Bob noticed that everyone seemed to be avoiding the empty chair next to Jeremy; in fact, Betsy brought a chair in from the next room and squeezed it in around the table to avoid sitting next to Jeremy. While everyone else chatted, Jeremy sat silently looking at his papers. Charles, however, seemed the center of the group. Everyone looked to Charles to talk first. You deduced he might be the informal leader of the employee group.

After that first meeting, Bob reviewed the performance evaluations for his staff. Jeremy's performance had been on the decline for the last year. The previous supervisor had rated Jeremy's performance as "exceeds expectations" one year ago. The last two quarterly reports showed a decline from "meets expectations" to "not meeting expectations" in the last evaluation period.

The evaluation reports included no specifics on Jeremy's performance to explain the decline in ratings. While the formal performance evaluations contained few clues about Jeremy's performance and why it was lagging, there was a handwritten note on a piece of paper clipped to the most recent evaluation that said: "Jeremy contends that Charles is taking reports compiled by Jeremy and destroying them. He claims that Charles is doing everything he can to make his life miserable."

After reading these materials, Bob kept his eyes open to check on how Jeremy and Charles got along, but he never saw them interact and Jeremy kept mostly to himself and didn't socialize with others in the office.

Discussion Question

1. How should the supervisor proceed with this situation?

8

Effective Communication in the Intercultural Workplace

Public servants cannot choose who they serve.

Cultural Knowledge and Public Administration

In the last fifty years, attention to diversity in the public sector has matured from reluctant acquiescence of regulations aimed at stopping exclusion of those in protected classes to a place of more genuine appreciation for diversity and culture. Borrego and Johnson (2012) commented: "Cultural competence seems to imply an emphasis on race and ethnicity. Cultural competence, in the broadest sense of the term, also includes other diversities among them gender, sexual orientation, and social class and cultural characteristics" (p. 34).

As NASPAA, the accrediting body for schools and programs of public administration, moved to require more soft skills in its standards, debate emerged on what the term cultural competency means: Is diversity competence attitudinal or behavioral? Is cultural competence connected to social justice? What does diversity mean (gender, sex, race, ethnicity, disability, sexual orientation, national origin, age, class, religion, language)? No exact template for defining diversity or cultural competency (outside of the legal arena) has been established (see, for example, Carrizales 2010; Gordon et al. 2012; Grandey and Diamond 2010; Rice 2007; Rivera, Johnson, and Ward 2010). Even so, there seems to be some agreement that although diversity is a broad term, it is important for public administrators to acquire an understanding of others (with "other" being any group or culture different from one's own). While total understanding of every possible culture is unrealistic, learning about culture and diversity theory is a good starting point. With general knowledge in hand, the public manager can focus attention on a local region's unique culture and diversity mix.

The evolution of approaches in public management can be traced from

Table 8.1

Evolving Perspectives on Diversity and Culture

Legal	Diversity	Cultural Competence
Equal Employment Opportunity laws: Focus on "preventing discrimination based on characteristics such as race, color, religion, gender, national origin, ability and age" (Riccucci 2002, p. 2).	"Ability of top management to develop strategies as well as programs and policies to manage and accommodate diversity in their workplace" (Riccucci 2002, p. 2).	Managing diversity in the organization as well as developing skills about cultural communication, mentoring cross-cultural employees, setting performance standards for cultural competence and measuring cultural competence.
Affirmative Action: "proactive approach to redress past discrimination."		

legal-centered perspectives preventing discrimination to broader concerns with diversity and cultural competence (see Table 8.1). The approaches are not mutually exclusive, but, rather, cumulative.

General frameworks of cultural competency often include three dimensions: knowledge (about local or national demographics, policy and law, and/or social justice issues), attitudes (personal growth about bias based on self-reflection), and communication skills (intercultural skills and meaningful involvement with populations other than one's root family or culture). Borrego and Johnson (2012) assert that culturally competent middle managers will understand the importance of managing diversity and how cultural differences can affect organizational effectiveness at formal and informal levels. In addition, middle managers should cultivate four specific skills: (1) communicating in culturally competent ways, (2) mentoring cross-cultural employees, (3) setting performance standards for cultural competence, and (4) measuring cultural competence.

As the field of public administration has expanded its gaze to include diversity and culture, many scholars have responded. Several quality books emerged that focus on interracial issues and inclusion of protected classes (see, for example, Borrego and Johnson 2012; Norman-Major and Gooden 2012; Riccucci 2002). Rather than duplicate those efforts, this chapter accepts the challenge of providing a macro perspective on intercultural communication. Specifically, we address the imperative of diversity, overview intercultural communication theories, and present specific tools for situations in which cultural differences complicate the problem-solving process.

The Imperative of Diversity

Race has always been an important theme and point of conflict in the United States. Racial inequity occurs when a dominant group uses power to exclude others. Since the colonization of the continent, the United States was a white-dominated country, where the European-American majority advantaged itself over other groups—legally and socially. This is evident in the nation's history of slavery, segregation laws, and racially or ethnically based zoning ordinances. Federal civil rights laws passed in the 1960s and 1970s, as well as slowly changing cultural attitudes, continue to move the nation toward equality.

In spite of these legal and attitudinal advances, genuine differences continue to mar effective communication across the cultural divide. For example, the many tribes indigenous to the North American continent developed a unique array of cultural traditions and communicative behaviors that may mystify those who are less culturally sophisticated. If the cross-cultural aspect of negotiating with tribes is not recognized, state and federal employees will experience many frustrations. In addition, partnerships with tribal nations may be strained (Peroff 2011; Prindeville and La Tour 2012; Sachs 2011; Walker 2004). Another example of cultural difference within the United States comes from studies showing some black American men and women exhibit communication patterns influenced by the cultural worldview of their African ancestors and by a century of living in a racially oppressive country (see, for example, Jandt 2012). Supervisors who are unaware of these communication nuances are at a disadvantage in their ability to understand or motivate individual employees. Similar traps await supervisors with employees or public contact with any combination of cultural influences (European American, Native American, Hispanic American, Arab American, Asian American, and so forth).

Stereotypes and (sometimes unconscious) prejudices abound around race and ethnicity. Competent communicators realize that—regardless of intent—we are all biased by our cultural upbringing and ideas of social stratification. Cultural groups carry unconscious templates of how the "best" people look, talk, and dress. When someone's cultural ethnocentrism leads to feelings of higher status, that person may unconsciously

Figure 8.1   **Percent of U.S. Labor Force by Race and Hispanic or Latino Ethnicity, 2011 Annual Averages**

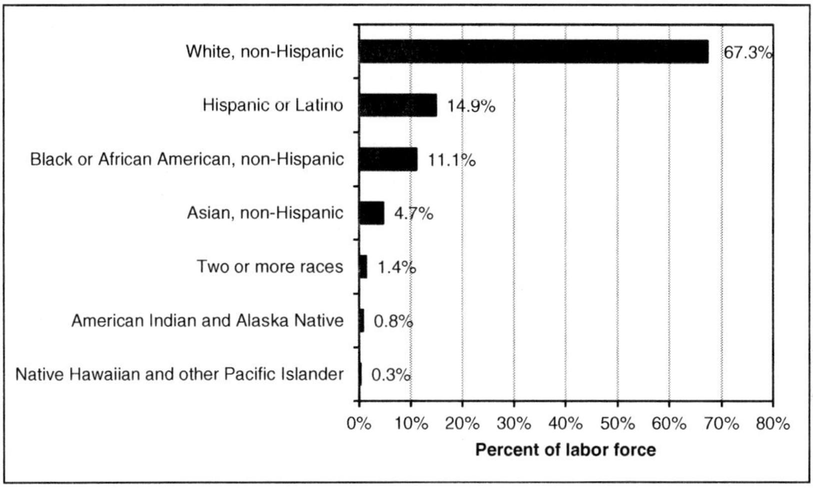

Source: U.S. Bureau of Labor Statistics (2010).

expect to be privileged over those who look or behave differently. Bias defeats the goal of providing fair and equal treatment to those served by public agencies. Other subtle stereotypes may creep into daily interactions. Even though statistics tell us many native Spanish speakers in the United States come from humble Mexican origins, assuming that anyone who speaks Spanish is from a family of farm workers is wrong. At best, such assumptions are overgeneralizations; for example, people who speak Spanish come from many countries around the world and from a variety of social positions.

Many agencies have acknowledged the positive benefits of hiring employees with diverse backgrounds rather than uniform characteristics. Programs in numerous agencies are models of diversity awareness or created policies with a genuine embrace between organizational values and cultivation of diversity. These policies cover everything from employee behavior, hiring practices, leadership cultivation, seeking the input of local populations, budgeting to support diversity efforts, thoughtful team composition, inclusion in reward systems, and extending diversity values to selection of vendors or external partners (see Borrego and Johnson 2012 for a review of federal agency model programs). Diversity statements have moved beyond mantras to avoid illegal discrimination against protected classes to acknowledgement that variety is valuable. The latter perspective approaches diversity for proactive reasons rather than just to avoid unwanted litigation.

Embracing diversity acknowledges protected classes as well as the many demographic groups residing in the country; for example, young and old, straight and gay, citizen and newcomer to the United States, poor and rich, dropouts and the highly educated, and so forth. Gordon and colleagues (2012) argue that the United States always has been a diverse country and it is the duty of public administrators to serve all of its diverse population. As Figure 8.1 indicates, the United States today is more diverse than ever before.

Intercultural Communication Theory

Culture is more than superficial differences about attire, food choices, or how close people stand to one another. *Culture* is a system of meaning and shared reality developed by a group (Ting-Toomey and Oetzel 2001). It is the deep structure from which values emerge, assumptions about the world are created, and perceptions form about what is right and wrong behavior.

To become culturally competent, individuals must understand the assumptions of their root culture and learn the assumptions of other cultures. To be culturally competent conflict communicators, an individual must understand how cultures vary in their basic assumptions about how to have conversations and how to manage problems. This chapter begins with an examination of how communication habits vary across cultures. Once a basic foundation of knowledge is created, individuals should become knowledgeable about the cultural groups in their specific service area. The culturally competent individual is mindful about stereotyping and "essentializing," the belief that everyone from a specific culture is essentially the same. All cultural groups exhibit variability in how specific individuals or subgroups subscribe to the dominant culture's tenets. For example, when you first meet an individual from China, a general knowledge of culture might suggest that individual would prefer indirect communication styles. This essentializing may be incorrect for a number of reasons; for example, an urban versus rural upbringing may have affected what someone learned about communication, the individual may have lived abroad since birth and was influenced by Western cultures, the family may have been more

Table 8.2

Collectivist and Individualistic Culture

More Individualistic	More Collectivist
Australia	Brazil
Belgium	China
Canada	Colombia
Denmark	Egypt
Finland	Greece
France	India
Germany	Japan
Great Britain	Kenya
Ireland	Korea
Israel	Mexico
Italy	Nigeria
Netherlands	Panama
New Zealand	Pakistan
Norway	Peru
South Africa	Saudi Arabia
Sweden	Thailand
Switzerland	Venezuela
United States	Vietnam

modern than traditional, and so forth. Cultural knowledge helps create a theory about how a specific individual from a particular culture may act. We must be ready to modify the theory when we know more about a specific person.

Three perspectives that help in understanding a culture's impact on communication behavior are Collectivism/Individualism, High/Low Context, and Hofstede's Cultural Value Dimensions. After exploring these theories, we will examine how managing interpersonal difficulties varies across cultures, along with implications of cultural differences in the public sector workplace.

Collectivism/Individualism

Is the individual more important than the group? Cultures vary on the answer. People reared in individualistic cultures are taught to look out for themselves, strive to achieve personal goals, develop a private identity, and use direct communication when solving problems. Those born to collectivist societies value their in-group, the family, school, or social group with whom they most identify; want to fit into the larger group rather than stick out by immodest demonstrations of how one is better

Table 8.3

Using Dissonant Feelings to Detect Cultural Clash

Behavior that causes a feeling of discomfort	European American ethnocentric interpretation	Other culture's possible intention or reaction
Not saying Yes or No to an issue	You are indecisive	I am showing respect and deference to authority
Staring and direct eye contact	I am showing connection	You are being impolite or aggressive
Having a close distance when conversing	Standing too close is a sign of aggression	Standing close is a sign of inclusion
Not indicating when one does not understand	You have low self-esteem	I am showing respect for authority
Smiling when receiving bad news	You are showing contempt or disrespect	I am embarrassed about the situation

Source: Adapted from Prince and Hoppe (2004).

than others; have a "we" identity; and strive to solve problems in ways that will not embarrass anyone.

When an athlete from the United States loses an Olympic event because of a mistake, that athlete will respond in interviews saying: "I will do better next time." Athletes from a collectivist culture may apologize for the error, feeling that they disgraced their homeland. In the workplace, wanting to know precisely who made a specific mistake on a report is not unusual; in a collectivist group, members might close ranks to protect each other from embarrassment and accept collective responsibility. Researchers nuance the individualistic and collectivist cultures in different ways, but countries can roughly be divided along the pathways exhibited in Table 8.2.

In collectivist cultures, in-groups are important enough to warrant more discussion. An in-group is the subset of the larger culture with whom one identifies. The darker nature of in-groups is the perception of outsiders as members of the out-group. Out-group individuals may be viewed as being of lesser value and may be treated more harshly than in-group affiliates, even though all are from the same root culture. Out-groups are the great "them," who are different from "us." Overgeneralizations are a common misperception of collectivist cultures, for example the belief that all Southeast Asian peoples are collectivist toward each other. The many varied cultures in one part of the world cannot be easily grouped into a uniform lump. In reality, the various Southeast Asian peoples prefer the in-group of their specific local culture, family, school, or other tightly associated affiliations. Likewise, the in-group of a workplace may divide along racial, gender, class, or ethnic lines or an in-group may form across organizational functions—field workers versus management (Nkomo 2010). Five behaviors are believed to trigger employees to think in social identity terms (in- vs. out-group) rather than in organizational citizen terms: Differential treatment across groups; treating the values of one groups as "right" and another groups as "wrong"; forcing assimilation to the dominant culture rather than allowing individual expression; humiliation; and contact with individuals who are different (Ruderman and Chrobot-Mason 2010). The latter item is ironic, as contact among diverse groups is advocated as a means of fostering familiarity. Yet initial contact may trigger social identity behaviors and conflict. Clear messages from leaders about the organization's value of diversity are one way of ameliorating the effects of social identity in the workplace.

High/Low Context Cultures

How do individuals interpret the meaning of what is said during a conversation? Cultures have developed unique ways to answer this question. Those in low-context cultures believe the meaning of a message is in the words spoken and people should directly say what they mean (Hall 1976). Without knowledge of other possibilities, the low-context individualist may think: "How could you possibly communicate any other way? How can you know what is going on if no one tells you?" Most European Americans are mystified by the possibility of alternate ways of interpreting the world—believing the words uttered are the most important part of a conversation.

For individuals from high-context cultures the words spoken may be the least important part of a conversation, as meaning arises from the situation or relationship. Because everyone in a high-context cultural group knows the same stories and has the same expectation about how to act in social situations, messages can be communicated through subtle gestures, stories, metaphors, or even the absence of speech—nuances that frequently are missed by those from low-context cultures. For example, in some cultures a sign of social disapproval can be expressed by a quick downward smile expression; no words need to be spoken. Instead of telling an employee that he is being too pushy, a manager might make a casual reference to a folklore story of an overly ambitious prince who ultimately was eaten by a dragon. In a high-context culture, the moral and the message to "back off" are clear.

It is useful when studying high/low cultures to understand that non-verbal communication is interpreted by cultures in unique ways. For example, some cultures use many facial expressions and others do not. A smile may show happiness in some contexts and embarrassment in others, depending on the culture. The up-and-down nod that means "yes" in one culture may mean "no" elsewhere. Personal space—the invisible comfort zone around one's body—varies from culture to culture. Even time can be experienced differently. Monochronic time describes a world in which time is sequential, exact, and appointments are sacred. Cultures that view time as polychronic experience it as circular and more flexible. In these cultures, appointment times are a general starting point rather than an exact expectation.

Hofstede's Cultural Value Dimensions

Dutch social psychologist Geert Hofstede developed a popular typology of cultures based on five dimensions: Power Distance, Individualism, Masculinity, Uncertainty Avoidance, and Long-Term Orientation (The Hofstede Center 2013).

The Individualism/Collectivism dimension (IDV) is identical to the concept discussed earlier in this chapter. The higher the individualism score the more "me" oriented the culture. The United States has the highest IDV score among countries categorized; Taiwan has the lowest.

Power Distance (PDI) describes a culture's expectations when one individual has more power than another or inequities exist in social status. It uses indicators such as how respect is shown for elders or those in positions of responsibility (teachers or supervisors). The lower the power distance, the more egalitarian the society. Higher PDI scores indicate a country comfortable with power inequities. Malaysia has the highest PDI ranking; Ireland has the lowest. In a high PDI culture, employees typically expect orders from supervisors and do not question instructions.

Masculinity (MAS) refers to the degree of competitive spirit versus compassion a culture evidences, with the original conceptualization of the category aligning these values with gendered stereotypes. For Hofstede, masculine cultures value competition (mostly for men) and show low compassion for the powerless. Feminine cultures value cooperation, nurturing, and caring for others who are less able. The highest MAS nation is Japan; Costa Rica is lowest.

The Uncertainty Avoidance Index measures tolerance for ambiguity and change. If people are uncomfortable in unstructured situations and have a low tolerance for different opinions, the culture is high in uncertainty avoidance. Uncertainty manifests during change. Some cultures see a problem and move quickly to change the situation; other cultures may think that situations should be accepted rather than confronted (Society for Human Resources Management 2008). Japan is the nation with the highest uncertainty avoidance score.

The final dimension, of Long-Term Orientation, is less well developed than the others. It describes a cultures' view of time as it relates to values. Those with a longer-term perspective esteem perseverance to overcome big problems and what happens today may be remembered for generations. Short-term perspectives may focus more on immediate reciprocity. China is highest in Long-Term Orientation.

Cultural Views of Problem Solving

Theories help reveal how people perceive problems and want to solve them based on a culture's values and preferred communication style. For example, a subordinate from a high power distance culture may not point out flaws in a plan to superiors or contribute during meetings, feeling that listening and obeying are important actions for individuals of his or her rank. Culture affects how people approach problem solving. The following section focuses on how different cultures enact interpersonal conflict strategies.

Intercultural Conflict Style

Hammer (2005) views a culture's preferred communication behaviors converging during interpersonal conflict in two important ways: how the disagreement is expressed and how emotion is expressed. Disagreement can be expressed directly or indirectly. Individuals from cultures preferring direct expression are comfortable with speaking to the person with whom an issue arises, will give direct answers to direct questions, and believe it's important to speak one's mind. Those from indirect cultures are uncomfortable with confrontation, feel embarrassed at direct questions, and may answer direct questions with ambiguous answers or a denial that there is a problem.

Figure 8.2 **Intercultural Conflict Styles**

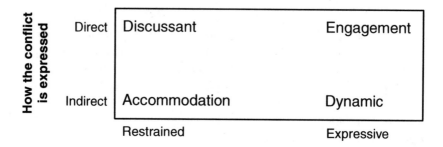

How emotion is expressed

The second dimension in Hammer's culture and conflict model is how emotions are expressed. Expressive cultures use expansive gestures, show passion for a topic with loud tones of voice, and let their feelings out. Other cultures are restrained—keeping personal emotions inside through minimal emotional displays and low tones. The dimensions of how disagreement is expressed and how emotions are displayed join to form four styles of intercultural conflict: discussant, engagement, dynamic, and accommodation (see Figure 8.2).

Cultures with a discussant style prefer direct communication and restrained emotions. Engagement cultures are expressive in emotion and direct in speech. Dynamic cultures actively express emotions and use indirect problem-solving methods. Accommodation cultures exhibit indirect problem-solving methods and restrained emotions. Hammer's work in typing cultures across the world led to the identification of Northern Europeans and United States whites as discussant style users. African Americans, Russians, Greeks, and southern Europeans generally exhibit engagement styles. The Arab world uses a dynamic approach. Accommodation styles are preferred in Japan, Southeast Asia, and among many Native American groups.

Imagine a social worker from a discussant culture meeting with an engagement culture family who does not understand why the "government" is coming to their home. The engagement individuals may speak loudly, gesture exuberantly, and use very passionate tones of voice. The social worker unaware of cultural differences may find this behavior threatening. When the same social worker visits an accommodation-style family, they may be indirect in stating problems—leaving the employee with the false interpretation that everything is fine and no services are needed.

Influences of Culture on Communication

Whether one talks about an issue, how one talks about it, when during a conversation substantive issues are broached, and how expressive one is about emotions vary across cultures. This variety has implications for the workplace and serving the public. For example, a lack of eye contact may be an indicator of respect in one culture and an indicator of lying in another. Culture of origin may affect how employees or clients sequence the timing of work or feel more or less urgency about tasks. European Americans, for example, focus on punctuality, whereas cultures with a more diffuse time sense do not. This mismatch may lead to one person being seen as too pushy and the other as disorganized or "late" in meeting deadlines (Farmer and Seers 2004).

Recognizing that some citizens will be reticent to discuss the real issue at the beginning of a conversation is important knowledge—especially to busy state or federal employees who would prefer that people come directly to the point. Cai and Fink explain: "Because individualist cultures rely on low context communication (i.e., meaning is explicit in the content of the verbal message), verbal expression of conflict may be normative. On the other hand, because collectivist cultures rely on high context communication (i.e., meanings are implicit within the context and relationship in which the communication takes place), verbal expression of conflict may be deviant" (2002, p. 83).

Guy and Newman (2010) claim: "Moving away from the industrial era treatment of individual workers as interchangeable parts, we now know that in service work, the person-to-person exchange is the human capital that determines how citizens feel about government" (p. 149). Likewise, we now know that citizens are not interchangeable or uniform in their cultural and communication expectations and abilities. It is incumbent upon the conflict-competent public employee to learn how to interact with those they are mandated to serve.

One of the challenges for many employees is recognition in a specific encounter that culture may be causing difficulties in communication. Prince and Hoppe (2004) suggest using feelings of discomfort as a way to recognize that something cultural might be occurring and then adapt behaviors accordingly or seek help (see Table 8.3, p. 126).

Influences of Culture on Management Style

It is not surprising after learning about cultural variability that management styles also can be culturally nuanced. For example, Ting-Toomey and Oetzel (2001) identify four primary cultural management styles that emerge when the individual/collectivist culture dimension is combined with the power distance dimension: impartial, status achievement, benevolent, and communal.

Impartial managers are higher in individualism and favor smaller power distance—meaning the manager values freedom of action and treating everyone the same within an organization. These managers generally deal with issues directly and expect employees to tell them when something is wrong. Employees may make suggestions to the supervisor without causing offense and participation may be demanded of employees. Employees (including those from root cultures with an indirect style or a large power distance) who do not participate may be perceived as standoffish, withdrawn, or not carrying their weight within the organization. When difficulties arise, the manager might use impartial rules or procedures as the criteria for solving the problem. The impartial approach is common to managers from Australia, Canada, Scandinavia, Germany, Israel, the United States, and the United Kingdom.

Status achievement managers also rank high on individualism, but prefer large power distance, meaning they are independent and believe they have earned status through the achievement of a management position. Because of their status achievement, these managers expect employees to be deferential. When problems arise, the manager will state what he or she wants to happen and expect the employees to follow directions without dissent. Managers from France, Italy, and some from the United States and the United Kingdom enact the status achievement style.

Benevolent managers come from collectivist cultures with large power distance. These managers feel interdependent with others in the organization, but have a higher status than their subordinates. These values result in managers believing they should take care of their employees as they would in an extended family, with everyone in the organization accepting different treatment depending on their place within the organization. Conflicts will be expressed indirectly, if at all, as harmony within the group is of primary importance. Managers are expected to protect their subordinates and subordinates are expected to anticipate the desires of the managers. Benevolent managers are common in Latin and South America, Asia, India, most Arab countries, and most of Africa.

The *communal* manager is both collectivist and has small power distance, common only to Costa Rica. These leaders see themselves as part of a larger group and at the same level as other employees. They have a preference for cooperative management and equal distribution of rewards across the organization.

One implication of differences in manager and employee styles arises during performance reviews. When attempting to foster engagement and motivate employees, Macey and colleagues (2009) suggest describing desired specific behaviors (i.e., "I would like everyone to make comments about how the work effort can be improved") rather than using personality judging statements ("You all should be more enthusiastic about your work"). Until employees are enculturated and trained in how to behave at a specific agency, the supervisor may need to coach individuals on the nuances of communication practices. Guy and Newman's advice should be considered. "Newcomers carry with them their nascent view of how things should be. Until they internalize the norms of the agency culture, their employment expectations will be driven by their preemployment expectations" (2010, p. 156).

Case: Refugees and the Library

You are the director of libraries for a medium-sized city (population 200,000) located in the central United States. In the last five years the Agency for New Americans, a nonprofit that partners with the U.S. Department of State, has resettled more than 2,000 refugees from Burundi who were fleeing ethnic violence in their home country. The refugees are encouraged by the nonprofit assisting them with resettlement to use the library and many are frequent visitors. The brightly colored African dresses, dark skin, and unfamiliar language set these patrons apart from the historically white population.

You have noticed that many longtime library patrons are staring at the refugees. Others appear wary of the newcomers. Some of the staff seem frustrated at the accented English these patrons speak. As you review the recent additions to the suggestion box, you note a couple of comments wondering why the refugee women always bring so many children into the library. One citizen wondered if it was "right" for the library to allow "checkout privileges" to people who "aren't from here."

Discussion Questions

1. What role can or should the library system play in helping the refugees adjust to their new home?
2. What steps might the library take to help staff and citizens interact more easily?

9

Dynamic Public Speaking

A presentation that goes well can be extremely fulfilling for both you and the audience, and it might even help your career. Some say that we "are born for meaning" and live for self-expression and an opportunity to share that which we feel is important. If you are lucky, you're in a job that you feel passionate about. If so, then it's with excitement that you look forward to the possibility of sharing your expertise—your story—with others. Few things can be more rewarding than connecting with someone by teaching something new, or sharing that which you feel is very important with others.
—Garr Reynolds, *Presentation Zen*

Speaking in the Public Sector

Most people are afraid of public speaking. A remarkable poll once found that Americans ranked speaking in public more fearful than death. Beginning speakers can be comforted by this truism: Audiences care more about how the message affects them than they care about the speaker. When presenters become overly focused on their appearance or what others think of them, they may fail the overarching goal of delivering an important message. As long as a speaker has a minimum level of presentational ability, audiences typically are more forgiving of foibles than speakers believe. Delivery matters, but it is rarely the most important variable in speaker success or failure.

Fulfilling two goals should consume the attention of those in the public sector who give presentations:

1. The content should be tailored to fit the audience's informational needs
2. The speaker should emphasize personal strengths and minimize weaknesses

There is a plethora of public speaking handbooks that expand on the details of speech writing and speech making. This chapter identifies basic principles of speaking and how they can be adapted to public sector employees' needs.

Matching the Purpose to the Audience

Knowing Your Purpose

Beginners frequently err in their preparation by viewing a speech as a basket of data to be conveyed. Baskets of data rarely enthrall listeners. Audiences prefer a purposeful message that is laser focused on a specific goal. Speakers must know their personal and organizational purpose to justify asking for the listeners' time and attention.

In general, messages carry a primary purpose of informing, persuading, or entertaining (the latter rarely is appropriate for public sector employees). Situations also may be rituals that demand specific types of messages—accolades for award winners, congratulations during celebrations, and so forth. In the public sector, messages also may carry the purpose to inoculate audiences against misinformation or bad science popularized on the Internet. Other presentational situations may involve training employees or volunteers. Training is a specialized type of speaking that is not addressed in this chapter.

Analyzing the Audience

Understanding the people in a specific audience and being able to respond strategically requires answering five key questions.

1. Who Is the Real Audience?

Deducing the audience of a message may be complex or simple. When briefing staff on a new project, department employees are the *primary audience*. When informing key stakeholders about a policy change, the individuals in the room at the time of a presentation may or may not be the only important listeners. Those who attend the speech may report to others who are important decision makers (a *secondary audience*). The same principle applies to written memos: one must consider all the potential readers when crafting a memo (or e-mail). For example, how a report is framed may vary depending on the recipient's preferences for details, patience with lengthy messages, or level of sophistication about the topic. An audience's expectations and feelings of message appropriateness will impact their acceptance.

Any speaking occasion has the potential for multiple audiences, some in the room, others viewing approved or unofficial recordings of the event, and a few who will hear about the message secondhand. People often learn about a speech through informal communication backchannels. Speakers always should consider who the most important listeners are and craft the speech both for those in the room at the time and for important listeners who are not physically present. Ignoring either audience is a tactical mistake. A speaker who is too frank because everyone in the audience is a friend is soon to be disappointed. The public employee should assume anyone in the agency or the public might learn about what was said. Whenever a speaker begins a sentence with "just between us here in the room," trouble is sure to follow.

To effectively adapt a message to an audience, one must understand its members. Audiences are not uniform in background or opinion. Standard questions help discover important similarities or differences among audience members. The answers help the speaker make tactical choices when crafting the speech.

2. What Are the Audience Demographics?

Demographics are relatively stable characteristics such as age, gender, religion, education, income, or political affiliation. When an audience has relatively uniform demographic characteristics, the speaker can focus on specific tactics. While one must be careful of stereotyping, certain predictions can be made based on demographics. For example, young, unemployed individuals probably are not very interested in how to purchase a burial plot in a public cemetery. Each age cohort has different life experiences, knowledge, and reference points (see Chapter 5). Comparing current events to civil rights protests in the 1960s may be impactful with audiences from the boomer age group, yet be relatively meaningless to Generation X listeners who view the 1960s as ancient history.

Many audiences will be mixed in their demographic composition. These groups require the additional work of adding examples that appeal to each segment of the audience rather than focusing on one group at the expense of another.

3. What Does the Audience Know About the Topic?

Listeners will vary in their sophistication about the topic. For a general audience, assume there will be varying levels of knowledge. Tactically, this means any acronyms of the trade or technical terms should be defined rather than assuming everyone knows the agency's jargon. For example, when the audience is composed of midcareer scientists, the speaker can use evidence that will be meaningful to data-oriented, sophisticated listeners. For a general high school audience, the speaker would choose fewer technical examples and more analogies, general examples, or translations of statistical data.

Speakers also should be curious about how the audience views the topic and the occasion: favorable, neutral, or hostile. Did the audience choose to voluntarily attend the speech or are they captives required to attend? Audience mood can have extreme impacts on speaker choices.

4. What Is the Speech Purpose in Relationship to the Audience?

Generally, public employees speak to inform. Sometimes, they may speak to persuade or advocate. It is important for public employees to remember their role when speaking, so as not to stray into inappropriate advocacy or political speech.

5. What Does the Audience Know About the Speaker?

Is the speaker a familiar face or name to the audience? Does the audience already find the speaker credible? If unknown, speakers must make a connection to the listeners early in the address. Credibility needs to be bolstered, either through an introducer's words or by the speaker's comments and demeanor. Touting one's credibility in a speech is a delicate matter. One cannot directly say: "Listen to me because I am an expert." Blunt statements may be perceived as egotistical. Instead, speakers suavely interject credibility-building statements: "In my fifteen years working as a scientist in the water management arena, I've had a chance to talk to many people throughout the country."

Aristotle's comments about credibility ring true centuries after he wrote his public speaking treatise *The Rhetoric*. Credibility is not inborn. It can be developed from a virtuous life and derive from the appearance of knowledge about the topic, high moral character, and good will toward the audience (Kennedy 1991). Modern research adds elements such as trustworthiness or dynamism as credibility-building factors.

Techniques to enhance personal credibility within the speech include: using sources reputable to the audience, selecting phrases that invoke values of the group, choosing inclusive pronouns to show affinity with listeners ("we" and "our"), being introduced by a person esteemed by the audience, demonstrating preparedness, and managing small difficulties well. For example, one of the authors has experienced many crises during presentations—having visual aids catch on fire, heckling, audience members' beepers all going off at the same time, falling off the stage, and having to wear sneakers with formal clothing. When the speaker manages these situations with aplomb or links the difficulty to the message, credibility soars.

Organizing the Message

Organization is a technical skill. A speech with transparent organization gives the impression of thoughtfulness and raises the speaker's credibility. In general, follow the steps discussed in this section. Planning is not done in the same order as the address is spoken. For example, writing the introduction section often occurs last in the preparation process, not first.

Start with a Goal Statement

What is the goal for the speech? The goal statement describes what the audience will know, think, or be able to do at the end of the address. Write the goal on the top of the planning outline. When the speech plan is completed, check the content against the goal statement to ensure that the focus has not drifted.

> Goal: At the end of my speech, the audience will be able to compare the five locations for the new sanitary landfill.

Convert the goal statement into a speech thesis to be shared with the audience.

> Speech Thesis: Today, let's take a look at the five locations the county has researched for the new sanitary landfill.

Select the Essential Key Points

Given the goal of the speech, what content is critical? Many possible points could be emphasized in a briefing about a new sanitary landfill. For example, an occasion could require an explication of the process the county used in locating the areas or a description of the five locations. Depending on the time available and the dynamics of the occasion, other key points might be more important, such as the pros and cons of each proposed site, history of the old facility, or how the public could be further involved in the decisions. After the essential points have been selected, write the preview of what the speech will include. The preview is a contract with the audience. It tells listeners what to expect from the rest of the speech. Content should not stray from the promised focus and should be organized under the same labels to make it easier for the audience to follow.

> Preview: Today, we'll have time to take a look at two aspects of the new sanitary landfill plan: How the county selected the five sites and the pros and cons of each of the five locations.

Provide Details and Evidence for Each Main Point

For each main point, identify what information is most important. For example, to understand the process the county used in arriving at its proposed sites, what do people need to know? The details of the answer create the realm of possibilities for the content of that section.

There may be data gathered for the speech that does not fit into one of the main points. This information is set aside rather than shoehorned into a bad fit. A competent speaker will have more knowledge about the topic than is shared in any one speech.

Once a list of possible content is established, a natural order for the information should emerge. Are the ideas about the five proposed sites best expressed chronologically (in time order of selection), spatially (by location on a map), by size (largest to smallest), or alphabetically (ordered by name)? Sometimes content is organized topically (familiar subdivisions), by cause and effect, or by problem and solution.

Ideally, each major statement in the speech is supported by evidence. Evidence can be as dry as the vast wastelands on Mars. Savvy speakers adapt evidence (without altering its veracity) to make it more interesting for a specific audience. Logical evidence (statistics, testimony, example, analogy) varies in quality and is only as potent as the credibility given to it by the listeners. In general, break difficult to understand evidence into bits the audience can comprehend. Instead of stating that 40,000 households use the garbage service each week producing 1,000,000 tons of refuse each year, translate the numbers into units the audience can understand: "If you lined up all of those green trucks to represent their trips to the landfill each month, they would stretch from here to Denver and back—seven times!"

For messages to be effective and credible, evidence should be double-checked—it is easy to misread statistical reports or make errors when copying from them. Ideally, a second person will assist with fact verification to certify the accuracy of the content. The speaker should have the source documentation of data used in the speech available to share if requested after the speech concludes. A handout given to the audience as they exit can present the data in raw form if appropriate.

Add the Introduction Section

Once the content for the speech is determined, it is easier to write an opening line. There may be a *proem* (preliminary comment) before the planned opening. These spontaneous comments thank someone for the invitation to speak, show appreciation to the introducer, or remark about the surroundings. The main purpose of the planned introduction is to garner the audience's interest. Introductions typically are short and followed immediately by the thesis statement and the preview. Some of the many techniques to gain interest and attention are identified in Table 9.1.

Add the Conclusion Section

The conclusion must accomplish two tasks: restate your main idea one last time and let listeners know you are about to finish your address. The latter is necessary to avoid awkward situations in which the speaker finishes without the audience catching on that the last words have been spoken.

Begin the conclusion with an ending cue such as "In conclusion," "Finally," "To wrap everything up," "To end our time together today," or "As my last words." This cue introduces a brief concluding statement that summarizes the main points, restates the thesis, and/or ends with a

Table 9.1

Techniques for the Speech Introduction Section

Humor	Jokes are out, but humor is a great interest generating technique—if you are a funny person. If you are not comfortable relating a humorous story, avoid this technique! All stories, cartoons, or funny graphics must be linked to the topic and be universally inoffensive—not just inoffensive to those in the room. If you are not sure, avoid using humor.
Story/ Example	Start with a story or specific example that illustrates the topic.
Surprise	Present a startling statistic, uncover an interesting scale model, or project a fascinating picture.
Analogy	Tell a story that is comparable to the topic.
Familiar or interesting quotation	Quote someone the audience is likely to find credible. Avoid saying "quote" and "unquote" when using another source. Instead, pause before beginning and at the end of the quotation, then say something like: "These words from . . ."
Refer to the place or occasion	If possible, link the topic to the room decorations, location, audience composition, or nearby historic markers "Today we are meeting not far from the site where power was first generated from Niagara Falls. Today, we gather to discuss a new contender in the energy market—wind."

vision indicating what things may be like after the recommendations in the speech are adopted. Ideally, the last sentence is uttered with a tone of finality.

> So, we've taken a look at all five of the proposed sites for the sanitary landfill. As I wrap up this briefing, I look forward to your input so we can finish this project and keep those green trucks rolling out of town for decades to come.

Link It All Together

Once the speech plan is complete, audiences appreciate the addition of a few organizational refinements such as internal previews, transitional statements, and internal summaries. Transitions are phrases that carry one part of a speech to another.

An internal preview forecasts what is to follow within a subsection of the message:

There are five locations under consideration at this time: Greenwood, Briar Patch, Stinky Hollow, the Black Ravine, and Circle Pit.

Internal summaries wrap up a section before moving to the next and often are combined with transitional statements:

Now that we've looked at how the commissioners started this whole process for a new facility, let's take a look at the locations that are being considered.

Internal organizing statements help listeners follow the speaker's message and know what will happen next.

So, those are the three criteria for site selection—volume of material that can be handled, number of households affected nearby, and cost—now let's take a look at what happens in the next stage of the decision-making process.

Adding Interest

Based on audience analysis, the speaker makes one more sweep through the speech plan to add content that encourages continued listening. As one cartoon quipped: "As the speaker my job is to talk. As the audience, your job is to listen. Hopefully, you will not finish before I do." For mixed audiences, the goal is to include something for everyone without offending anyone. Select examples, use illustrative stories, translate statistics, graph numbers, create an analogy, make reference to the audience or the occasion, or add short quotations that a specific audience segment may find engaging. All such additions to the speech must be in good taste. Avoid anything that may be considered offensive or disrespectful.

Final Check: Does the Content Meet the Audience's Needs?

When the final draft is completed, one more step is prudent. Return to the overall goal that was noted at the beginning. Check to ensure that the final product fulfills the intended goal and is appropriate for the specific audience or occasion.

Tip: Don't say anything you are not willing to have broadcast worldwide in a YouTube video—even if you are among friends.

Dress for Success
Recommended Tips

Deciding what to wear when delivering a speech can be complicated. The general rule is to choose clothing one step more formal than what the audience is expected to wear. If the audience will be wearing suits, wear a high-quality suit. If the audience dresses in business casual, wear a suit or high-end business casual. If the audience is in work clothing, wear business casual. In general, avoid clothing with busy patterns that might distract the audience and cause them to focus on what you are wearing rather than what you are saying. Leisure and party attire rarely are appropriate when speaking as a representative of government.

Speech Delivery

Emphasize Presentational Strengths

Knowing that you have a well-crafted message can make all the difference in speech delivery. This section discusses the nonverbal track of a speech presentation. The target for mastery of speech delivery is to find a zone of relative confidence and comfort. The speaker must not come across as blasé and choreographed; puppetlike gestures should be avoided. Instead, focus on transforming any jitters into positive energy. For example, many speakers find benefit in taking the nervous energy at the beginning of a speech to create more volume, bigger gestures, or more vocal intensity. Audiences appreciate intensity more than timidity.

Use the Right Style of Notes

Beginning speakers are drawn to writing out the speech and reading it aloud, word for word (called manuscript style). However, most people do not do this well. To read a manuscript successfully, one must be familiar enough with the words to have some sustained eye contact with listeners. One must mark the manuscript on where to vary vocal pitch, emphasize a specific word, or pause for effect. Without refined technique, manuscript reading becomes a monotonous dirge and the audience may wonder why they have to be physically present—couldn't the speaker have just e-mailed the information out to everyone?

One of the authors witnessed the deadening effect of the manuscript delivery style in a speech given by a university official to 300 faculty members. Copies of the speech were provided at the door. Soon, almost everyone was silently reading along with the speaker, heads bowed. As the speaker turned a page, so did virtually the entire audience—creating a nice breeze in the stuffy auditorium. Because the speaker was wedded to the manuscript and the audience was looking down at their copies of the speech, only two of those attending the event noticed the kitten that walked onstage and sauntered around in front of the podium.

To avoid the traps of manuscript speaking, novices are better served with a partial manuscript or extemporaneous notes. The partial manuscript method splits the page vertically with the entire text on one side and key words on the other. One can speak from the key word outline extemporaneously and use the manuscript as a backup, if needed. The full manuscript portion should be marked with frequent places to look up at the audience. Also, underline words to stress vocally and indicate when to pause. When crafting a manuscript speech remember that conversational speech is less grammatically perfect than written communication. To please the ear, split infinitives and create shorter sentences. Practice the speech several times. Make changes to delete words you have trouble pronouncing and to enliven the address with vocal variety—changing the vocal pitch to emphasize words, pausing for dramatic effect, or speeding up/slowing down to create vocal contrast.

When handling the notes, pages should be numbered and left unbound. Only write on one side of each sheet. Using both sides can create two types of embarrassment: having audience members in the front row squinting to read the backside of the note pages and the speaker forgetting which side of the page he or she is on. When a page is done, slide it to the side rather than flipping it over noisily—particularly when using a podium microphone.

Allow Natural Gestures and Sincerity

A speech should sound sincere and the speaker should seem interested in the topic. When speakers focus on how nervous they feel, energy is drawn inward rather than pushed outward. The goal isn't to get rid of the speaker's butterflies; it is to make them fly in formation.

Begin the speech with greater volume than typically used in conversation to put the extra nervous energy to work. Focus on the desire to have the audience understand the message and set your energy free. Unclench the hands grasping the podium and they will start to make natural gestures. Beginning speakers are too focused on perfection and may wind up looking like cardboard cutouts. Specific gestures that are overly planned *look* overly planned. If you gesture when you converse, you will have gestures while speaking to a group as soon as you let your arms have freedom. In fact, when speaking to most groups, bigger gestures are preferred. Instead of restraining any natural gestures, make them bigger!

Another worry that speakers have concerns vocalized pauses—"um" or "er" sounds. Vocalized pauses are natural in conversation—the "um" says "I'm not yet ready to give up the conversational lead." The vocalized pause keeps others from starting their conversational turn. When speaking in public, audience members rarely jump in when the speaker pauses. So, vocalized pauses are not necessary. More credibility can be attained if the speaker can learn to be silent when the urge to "um" occurs, but a modest number of these vocalized pauses are acceptable to listeners. More problematic are age or cohort-based lingo and speech patterns, for example, saying "like" or "you know" in every other sentence—"It is, like, a large engineering challenge to look at all the places in the county where a sanitary landfill could be placed, you know."

The best advice for presentational style is to be your best self rather than try to emulate someone else. Audiences are adept at detecting insincerity and falseness.

> **Tip:** When speaking in a full room, only the people in the front row can see a seated speaker—stand up.

Make Eye Contact

If one remembers that the purpose for speaking is to foster understanding of an important message, it is easier to make eye contact with individual audience members. Ideally, every person in the audience should feel that the speaker glanced her or his way during the talk. If looking someone in the eye is difficult, look at foreheads or chins—close enough that listeners will feel the speaker's gaze. For large venues, look at each section of the room. Beginning speakers tend to overfocus on a few areas and completely ignore the rest of the room. Sometimes a friendly face or supportive listener grabs the speaker's attention. Sometimes the speaker gazes straight ahead and misses connecting with those sitting around the edges of the room. Make the effort to look around.

Practice

Practice rises above all of the other technical matters in speech writing and preparation. Many novices do not speak the message aloud or project their PowerPoint slides while practicing. As a consequence, the speaker and the audience are "hearing" the message for the first time together. Audiences deserve better. If it is important enough to prepare a speech in advance, it is important enough to practice the delivery of the message along with any visual aids to discover problems. During the speech is not the time to discover you can't pronounce a key term.

Visual Aids and PowerPoint Presentations

Many speakers have embraced PowerPoint and other presentational software with reckless abandon—spending hours crafting slides with beautiful sound-enhanced graphics that fly in and out of the frame. Sometimes that creative investment is worthwhile, but often the visual aids are too animated and distract from the real message. One speaker commented that he spent about ten hours making a chart with content that flew in from different directions and then animated the flow of an evaluation process. Audience members thought it was a lovely animation, but a shame that the words on the slide were too small to read.

The purpose of a visual aid is to enliven the presentation or illustrate something in ways that aren't possible with just words. It is important to remember that visual aids support a speech and do not substitute for the speaker's words. Visual aids form a second level of meaning that accompanies the verbal track. Common mistakes of PowerPoint presentations include using the presentation as giant note cards that the speaker reads word for word to the audience, putting too much detail on one slide, or designing slides that are unappealing to the eye. The following sections detail how to use the most common visual aids: posters, handouts, models, PowerPoint slides, and audiovisual clips.

Giving Public Testimony
Recommended Tips

When asked to provide information at a hearing, the request typically is for a briefing. Because hearing boards or commissions will take testimony from many sources, it is important to be content-efficient and within the time limit.

When preparing the testimony:

1. Acquire the rules and time limits for this specific hearing.
2. If possible, sign up for a time slot early in the agenda so the board is fresher and there is a lower probability that your opportunity to testify will be overrun by other events.
3. Time your presentation during practice sessions to be sure you do not run past the allowed limit. Being cut off by the chairperson reduces the credibility of the message.
4. Pay attention to the mistakes or success of those who precede you. Take advantage of the lessons they offer.

When giving the testimony:

1. State your name and position, who you represent, or your background. "My thanks to the council for this invitation to brief you on the contract processes used for snow plowing. My name is Jesse Rivera and I am the director of transportation for the city."
2. During the first two minutes, highlight the key message. Boards often suffer from listening fatigue during testimony or only skim the written proceedings.
3. If you have time, tell a compelling story. "Last December 28th, we experienced an unusual and record-breaking 23 inches of snow over a 15-hour period. At that time, the city owned 3 snowplows and our contingency plan for the maximum typical snowfall of 4 inches was to put the plows on 3 vehicles and pay the drivers overtime. Once the snowfall reached 6 inches, we knew we were in trouble and attempted to get assistance from the county. While they wanted to help, they also were overwhelmed. We began to subcontract to any company who had a plow in an attempt to keep traffic and commerce moving. This strategy was ineffective and expensive. Over the past summer, we investigated how other cities manage unusual and extreme snow situations and met with local citizens and business interests, as well as with other city departments. The details of our newly revised snow removal plan and contracting process are in Exhibits 1 and 2."

4. If appropriate summarize the risks and benefits of a proposed action.
5. Be civil.
6. Double verify the accuracy of data.
7. Summarize your main idea and thank the board for the opportunity when closing your comments.

On the other side of the coin, if you are a board member receiving testimony, the public and employees will appreciate your full attention. Avoid texting, reading other documents, taking phone calls, or napping while hearing testimony.

Posters and Display Boards

Posters typically are charts, pictures, graphs, or other data on large (2 x 3 feet), stiff backed material. With the advent of large format printers, poster creation has become easier and more economically viable. Commercially prepared display boards sometimes are created to highlight specific projects and used to present talking points during public meetings. Table 9.2 offers guidelines for creating posters and display boards.

Handouts

A good handout can save time and give the audience details too complicated for the speaker to cover in the allotted time. Handouts can be referred to during the speech or provided as a takeaway. During the speech, brief handouts could accompany specific content points. The downside of a handout is getting it to the audience at the appropriate moment without causing too much disruption. If the handout is given at the outset, many listeners will read it rather than listen to the speaker. If the handout is used at a specific time during the speech, assistance may be necessary to distribute the material to the audience quickly and efficiently. If a handout is complicated, different reading speeds of audience members may lose the attention of half the group.

Handouts that are copies of the speaker's PowerPoint slides can be useful or dreadful. When possible, ask listeners not to "read ahead" of you and instead draw their attention to specific content as necessary. For PowerPoint slide handouts, any more than three slides per page will lose too much detail in small print.

Table 9.2

Guidelines for Posters and Display Boards

Size	The font should be large enough to be read by the farthest audience member. For display boards at a conference, assume a 4 to 6 foot distance.
Precision	The details should be precise enough to be understood in a few moments rather than require deep processing.
Data-friendly	Statistics should be translated (via colorful graphs, pie charts, or other symbols) rather than presented in tables of raw numbers.
No early reveals	The poster should be covered until the speaker arrives at the point in the speech where the data is needed.
Visibility	The poster should be displayed so all audience members can see it.
Only one idea per poster	Too much detail is distracting.
An image trumps a thousand words	A combination of pictures and images is preferred to a poster with only words.
The graceful change	If multiple posters are used, the speaker should practice how to change from one to another gracefully and know where to put a poster when it is taken down.

Takeaway handouts can be particularly useful. When discussing a section of a report, tell listeners that material will be available at the exit for those who wish to study the data in more detail.

Audiovisual Clips

A brief audio or video clip can be very illustrative. Computer editing and presentation software programs have made these elements easier to use. Some criteria for audiovisual clips are listed in Table 9.3.

Models

Sometimes a model is helpful, for example, a small replica of a road grader considered for purchase or a scale model of a new subdivision. Geographic Information System (GIS) computer modeling can create wonderful illus-

Table 9.3

Guidelines for Audiovisual Clips

1. The clip must be as brief as possible.
2. The clip must be of sufficient quality when projected to be seen and heard by all audience members.
3. The speaker must ensure the technology/software can be projected with the equipment in the room.
4. The speaker must introduce the clip and foreshadow what to pay attention to.
5. The speaker must comment about the clip after it is played.

trations of spatial associations. Whether computer models are projected onto a screen or a physical model of an object is brought to the occasion, all audience members should be able to see and easily comprehend the object as the speaker explains it. Practice several times to gain competence with any physical objects that need to be manipulated. Even simple tasks like opening a bottle become complex in front of an audience; total competence at visual aid management is required to maximize credibility.

Presentational Software

Presentational software such as PowerPoint transformed speechmaking with its ease in creating effects and backgrounds. For the novice speaker, PowerPoint's allure can have mixed results. Cluttered backgrounds, small print, tiny graphs copied from reports, and fuzzy photographs all damage speaker credibility. At times, a single picture with no label is the best visual—the right image supports the message without distracting the audience. For example, a speech on road construction might be underscored by a slide of a congested intersection. A speech on innovation might feature a slide with a big question mark. In this sense, a projected slide can be thought of as the second track to support the speaker's spoken narrative.

Those using presentational slides should adhere to several foundational principles about color, balance, and continuity (see Table 9.4). In general, colors should be bright without clashing. Many software programs offer busy templates that are too dim, too exotic, or consume too much of the slide space.

Additionally, slides should be balanced. The eye prefers the top two-thirds of a defined space and elegant proportions. Putting too much on

---

Table 9.4

Visual Aid Design Principles

- Visual aids should add to the content rather than be the content.
- Only one idea per slide.
- If you must have a long list, create preview slides and utilize subsequent slides for details on each item or reveal one item at a time.
- Font 24 point size or larger.
- Avoid red/green colors and backgrounds (color blind individuals lose the contrast of red/green patterns).
- Avoid excessive use of flying in letters, dissolves, and other advanced features that do not serve a specific, content-emphasizing function.
- Use standard rather than exotic backgrounds.
- Less detail is better than too much clutter.
- Create easy to understand pie charts, bar charts, or other symbol representations rather than tables of numbers.
- Summarize data in colorful pullout pie charts or pictograph charts made with any of the available presentational software products.

---

a slide unbalances the content. Unharmonious arrangements with one side bigger than the other should be avoided. Likewise, viewers prefer continuity. Using the same theme throughout is preferred to frequent background changes. Headings, small icons, or other devices may be used to provide continuity among and across the slides in a presentation.

One additional challenge with presentational software is the gap between computer screen and projected images. The audience will not see exactly what the computer screen shows while one is composing the presentation. Colors fade or change to unattractive hues; edges of pictures disappear from the bottom of the screen. Test important presentations on location with the actual projection equipment. Sit in the back row while an assistant runs the slides. Can you read the words (font size), is the color pattern right for the room, will the bottom half of slides be concealed by the heads of audience members sitting toward the front of the room?

Plan to use the right mix of the three levels of information available with presentational software: slides projected for all to see, slide handouts (no more than three per page) for listeners to use as a reference during the address, and handouts that can be taken away (that are different from the slides). As Reynolds (2008) comments: "Handouts can set you free." Instead of including a deadening amount of specific detail when only one or two audience members care, provide the details in a takeaway handout.

Introducing Another Speaker

We may all be called upon to introduce a guest expert or speaker at some point in our careers. Introducing another speaker is a technical skill with specific requirements. Avoid the dark side of speaker introductions. Many introducers unintentionally say things that either detract from the speaker's credibility or make the situation awkward. There are several common pitfalls that should be avoided when introducing a speaker.

Some introducers are unintentionally patronizing ("I'm glad to introduce a little lady from the mayor's office"), which can trivialize the speaker's credibility or social standing. Introducers who do not adequately prepare may be vague about the speaker's topic ("I'm not sure what Kevin is speaking on today, but I'm sure it will be great"). The person "helping" the speaker sometimes starts before the speaker is ready ("So, here's Katarina—I'm sure she's around here somewhere—Oh, there she is"), which makes the speaker seem as if she was the one who was unprepared. Some introducers shuffle papers or move equipment that the speaker carefully prearranged, causing a delay or giving the impression that the speaker is disorganized. Partisan introducers may say negative things about the topic ("I'm not a big fan of endangered species designations myself, but we should give a listen anyway"). Finally, introducers might engage in any number of other negative behaviors or make unhelpful comments ("So, here's Maria. I'm sure she won't speak too long or be too boring").

A competent speaker introducer acknowledges that there is a job to be done to prepare the audience and support the speaker. The steps in Table 9.5 guide the novice introducer through the process.

After checking that the speaker is ready and the room is properly arranged, move to the front of the room, gather the audience's attention, and begin the introduction. In general, speak loudly to get attention and sound enthusiastic about the speaker and the topic. Look at the audience during the first line of the welcome.

Look at the speaker during the last line of the introduction to transfer the audience's attention to the speaker. If appropriate, lead the audience in applause to welcome the speaker to the stage.

Case: Telling the Public to Prepare for Disaster

As an assistant public affairs officer for the county's emergency preparedness department, you are scheduled to give three speeches to brief com-

Table 9.5

Guidelines for Introducing Another Speaker

1. Discover facts about the speaker
   • Correct pronunciation of his or her name
   • Minimal information about the speaker's credibility/position
   • Request a speaker's bio if available, but avoid reading it in its entirety
   • Consult with the speaker about your introduction so you don't use the same material the guest has planned for his or her opening
2. Collect information about the occasion or topic
   • What is the speaker's topic?
   • Why has this group gathered to listen to this speaker?
3. Help the speaker set up
   • Move extraneous chairs, equipment, used water glasses, or other possible distractions from the speaker's area
   • Erase the previous speaker's whiteboard notes or move other speaker's visual aids
   • Help the speaker set up equipment, visual aids, check microphones, load data onto a projection unit
   • Close doors if outside noise is distracting or open doors if it is too hot in the room
   • Inform the speaker of any time signals that will be used
   • Check with the speaker that he/she is ready before starting the introduction
4. Write an introduction that contains at least these basic elements:
   • Captures the audience's attention and hands it to the speaker
   • Welcomes the group to the occasion (if this is the first/only speaker)
   • States how the topic is of interest or important to the group
   • Conveys the speaker's credibility on the topic—unless it is a very formal occasion, listing one or two credibility items will suffice
   • Uses the speaker's name when asking the audience to welcome him/her to the stage

munity members about disaster preparedness. The core of the speech will cover the most common disasters likely to hit your county and steps that businesses, families, and individuals can take to prepare for those disasters. The most likely natural disasters in your area are floods and tornadoes. Homeland security also asked each county to prepare plans for a terrorist attack such as a bomb or an incident involving chemical or biological weapons. The three speeches you will deliver are to (1) a high school class; (2) the Chamber of Commerce; and (3) a neighborhood association.

Discussion Questions

1. Will you talk about all of the disasters to each audience?
2. How, if at all, should the three speeches differ in the level of detail?
3. What additional information might you need to prepare for the speeches?

10

Designing Effective Public Input Processes

Why Seek Input?

Public sector entities may gather the opinions of employees or the general public for several statutory or strategic reasons. Sometimes agency heads want employees to participate in setting standards for new policies (such as workplace respect) or to shock test proposed technical standards. Employees' input may be sought to discover their satisfaction level in their work or to pinpoint weaknesses in agency policies, practices, or leadership.

The public may be asked to participate because their input is required by law or because agencies wish citizens to feel invested in a decision. The public may have information that is not otherwise available to an agency. For example, the city of Portland, Maine, recently moved from a council election to a general election for mayor. Research indicated that other cities shouldered heavy costs from multiple run-off elections due to rules requiring the successful candidate have a majority of the votes. Citizen input was gathered in Portland on how to hold their mayoral election in a cost-effective manner. The result was a complex proposal for rank ordering a voter's ballot that often listed more than a dozen candidates. A computer program tested the ballots to see if a candidate acquired a majority on a first vote, then drop off the lowest ranked candidates and reran the same ballots with a rank-ordered formula. In the first election using this method, computers ran the ballots fourteen times until a winner emerged with a weighted majority (Koenig 2011). Follow-up input processes will assess the public's satisfaction with the new voting methodology.

Public processes also manifest a virtue of moderating the influences of cronyism and powerful stakeholder groups. When a collective opinion is gathered in ways that are perceived by the public as being open and fair, accountability is enhanced. Input provides a means for government agencies and nonprofits to assess if they are meeting real needs or missing the mark, as well as learn about the pending changes in their service areas.

Finally, public participation processes provide a means to educate the public. The exchange of information during a public meeting does not have to be one-way. The public can express opinions, content experts from an agency can educate citizens about science or technical realities, and agency heads or elected officials can inform the public about the legal and procedural constraints surrounding an issue.

Depending on the methods used, public participation processes may build consensus around a specific decision or foster public understanding of a problem's legal, financial, and technical constraints. Shirking opportunities for genuine public feedback or conducting an input process in a manner than is perceived as insincere can crush public trust and increase resistance to change. The more local and immediate the public process, the greater the probability that individuals will be interested (Wang 2001).

Bad Behaviors in Public Places

Bad behavior is nothing new, but the prevalence of incivility seems to be increasing. Passionate outbursts at public input sessions and planned protest to disrupt meetings are captured with increasing frequency on today's omnipresent electronic media. The negative invective during political campaigns seems to carry over to public meetings and other places intended for measured, deliberative processes. In the public forum, sometimes it is easy to discern the planned protest from the passionate outburst; sometimes it is not. When a theater group pretending to be audience members broke into song to object to the demise of the public option in the health care bill at an American Health Insurance Plans annual state issues conference, the protest was obvious, planned, and refined (Webster 2009). When a congressman yelled "you lie" at President Obama during a joint session or an individual in attendance at a public meeting screams invectives at a county commissioner, the incivility probably stems from a combination of passion about the topic and a momentary lapse of judgment. Regardless of the cause, many agree with Innes and Booher's (2000) conclusions that the traditional formats for legally required public input meetings are not working as well as they did in the past:

The traditional methods of public participation in government decision making simply do not work. They do not achieve genuine participation in planning or decisions; they do not provide significant information to public officials that makes a difference to their actions; they do not satisfy members of the public that they are being heard; they do not improve the decisions that agencies and public officials make; and they don't represent a broad spectrum of the public. Worse yet, they often antagonize the members of the public who do try to work through these methods. (p. 2)

Wang (2001) describes traditional public participation processes as including "public hearings, citizen forums, community or neighborhood meetings, community outreaches, citizen advisory groups, and individual citizen representation. Citizen surveys and focus groups, the Internet, and e-mail are also used" (p. 322). There is general concern that incivility may not be a passing fancy and is a threat to democratic processes and government attempts to foster communication with the public. Mutz and Reeves (2005) suggest that incivility may lead to general public negativity or lack of public participation by those who are put off by confrontational meetings.

> **Tip:** Never raise your voice no matter how much someone yells at you in a public forum. Leaders can't outyell or scream at an audience member. It just looks bad. Any time you come across as out of control, you look weak. It's fine to be passionate, and even allow your emotions to show, but screaming and yelling never works when you are in charge. (Adubato 2009)

The Significance of Incivility in Public Meeting

Civility, simply put, is the "way people treat each other with respect—even when they disagree" (Institute for Local Government 2003, p. 1). There are several reasons managers of public meetings should care about incivility. First, if incivility is a rising wave in society, it might be the kind that sinks all ships instead of raising them. Unrestrained incivility is believed to have a chilling effect on the public processes through which democracy functions. The ability to speak to or question government representatives at public meetings and to have one's opinions heard is stunted if shrill voices screaming negative messages overwhelm an event.

Table 10.1

Methods of Public Input

- Focus group
- Community outreach
- Citizen advisory group
- Individual citizen representation on boards
- Citizen group representation on commissions/boards
- Negotiated rulemaking
- Placing an e-mail feedback link on webpages
- Using other Internet means of seeking feedback
- Public hearings
- Citizen forums
- Community/neighborhood meeting
- Briefing panel
- Debate
- Input session
- Collaborative process
- Neighborhood meeting
- Survey

In addition to the possibility of halting a public process when incivility goes too far, there may be a chilling effect if the general public fears that an event will "go negative." A study of incivility in the workplace found that when there was rudeness at work, 48 percent of bystanders reduced their work, 47 percent decrease their time at work, 66 percent said their performance declined, 80 percent lost work time worrying about the incident, 63 percent lost time avoiding the offender, and 78 percent said their commitment to the organization was lessened (Porath and Pearson 2009). If the distaste for rudeness at work also applies to public occasions, some members of the public will decline invitations or not participate in public meetings with a history of too much incivility. In sum, if shrill voices can drive away more moderate opinion, the intent of an open public process may be subverted.

Second, those who convene public meetings should care because incivility creates a meeting management and security issue. How should protest be handled? Must security personnel be present? What level of protest is legitimate and what level of protest is too much? These and other questions must be addressed as part of event planning. Some forms of public protest are legitimate outcries against those who regulate or govern the public. Those who manage public meetings must balance between a sometimes outraged public's need to vent and the mandate to carry on with the business of governing.

The third reason to care about incivility is related to the second. It is probable that some incivility in specific cases arises because the wrong process has been used. If members of the public feel that nobody has listened or that decisions already have been made, emotions may run high—and for good reason.

Strategies to Counter Incivility

What can be done when one is faced with an angry public? Susskind and Field, who are expert facilitators in large multiparty conflict, conclude: "We believe that the solution lies in acting in a trustworthy fashion, sharing information, and engaging in joint fact-finding and collaborative problem-solving" (2012, p. 12). While no single idea will be appropriate in all contexts, the following section presents a menu of strategies for the planner of public meetings and public input processes.

Decision-Making Style Transparency

The public meeting format needs to be transparent about how decisions will be made and the meeting agenda should be designed to match the decision style. The command, confer, convene, and concede framework is helpful for leaders considering where input fits into the decision-making process. In the command style, leaders make decisions alone and tell stakeholders the outcome. Confer style encompasses decision makers asking the opinions of others. Conferring can be the systematic use of public meetings, casual conversation with whomever decision makers bump into, or a discussion among a small group of stakeholders or trusted advisors (also called consulting; see Van Wart 2011). In the convening framework, a more formal meeting structure, subcommittee, or task force is commissioned to learn about a problem, analyze it, and make recommendations. Finally, the concede method occurs when decision makers give authority to someone else or to a convened group. For all styles, expectation management is the key. The public who attends a meeting expecting to discuss a pending decision will be upset if what occurs is a presentation about a command decision that already has been made.

Choosing the Right Format

The chosen format of a public meeting should consider several variables: (1) The decision-making format, (2) the probable interest of the public

---

Table 10.2

Planning the Public Meeting

1. What is the purpose of the meeting?
2. Are there specific stakeholders who should be invited or notified?
3. What is the budget for the event?
4. How can you build relationships with participants in advance of the meeting?
5. What is the level of public interest/indignation/outrage?
6. What meeting space (size, location, configuration) will be best?
7. What should the specific agenda be for the meeting?
8. What format should be offered to structure the public participation?
9. Who is the right person with the needed skills to facilitate the meeting?
10. What could go wrong? What is the contingency plan?
11. What method(s) should or must be used to advertise the opportunity?
12. How can the Internet or social media be used to advertise or gain additional input?
13. What do you tell the public will happen to their input?
14. Who will make the ultimate decisions (command, confer, convene, or concede model)?

---

in the issue—how many people are likely to attend, (3) the number and variety of stakeholders, (4) the emotional tone of the debate on the issue thus far and its potential for volubility, and (5) laws and regulations constraining what may be done.

In all formats, people need to feel heard and to feel safe. Sandman (2008) describes seeking the sweet spot of public participation—people are interested in the issue, but are neither outraged nor apathetic. The format for public meetings should be suited to what the issue evokes: apathy, reasoned deliberation, or outrage.

Some formats are designed so that those in attendance are not permitted to speak. Briefings and panels typically have invited speakers who inform the public and then take questions or comments from the floor. If the topic is "hot," members of the public may bring their passion to the event and feel either muzzled by the format or offended by the facts presented by those they oppose. If a panel or briefing format is chosen, publicity must clearly indicate it is "informational" and whether the general public will have any opportunity to ask questions or participate in other ways. The public is particularly resistant to briefings if there is a perception that decisions were made before opportunities for public participation (command decision style). The word "perception" is important—the public must not only be given information on the nature of an event (participatory or not) but perceive that they were given sufficient notice. Merely checking off statutory or rule obligations to advertise public meetings often is insufficient.

Conversely, some formats are too vulnerable to co-option by organized interest groups. If prior registration is required to speak at a meeting or give public testimony, the most organized group(s) will take all the available slots. In light of the fact that information is available on the Internet on how to disrupt public meetings, thoughtfulness in preparation choices is advisable.

Separate Information from Decision Making. During the initial phase, seek public input on what people would like to know about the issue. After analyzing the public's need for information, select the science or policy topics for the session. After the briefings, offer public opinion input or a venting session. Formats that only suppress public outrage do not make the outrage disappear.

Arrange a Venting Session. If people are outraged, one form of input is to ask for their objections and grievances. Listen respectfully. Venting is a part of the process and should not be seen as always counter to the process of governance (see Sandman 2008).

Use a Strong Moderator. A strong moderator is more effective than a novice. For example, the moderator can reframe a question so an expert is responding to a general issue rather than to an individual's specific (and perhaps awkward) question.

Provide Information via Electronic Media. Social media can provide a channel for eliciting questions, giving briefings, or soliciting opinion— make it clear at each stage what type of information is being solicited. Wang (2001) found that 81 percent of cities surveyed used the Internet to sign up and advertise speakers. Use of the Internet can include opportunities for giving input on an agency's website.

Select a Collaborative Process. It is beyond the scope of this chapter to present collaborative processes in detail. However, when the decision is complex, time is available, and many stakeholders have opposing opinions, a collaborative process may be appropriate. Those who engage in longer-term problem solving have the opportunity to learn about all sides of an issue and understand the value of compromise (Daniels and

Table 10.3

Charrette Components

- Definition of the issue to be resolved
- Analysis of the problem and alternative approaches to solutions
- Assignment of small groups to clarify issues
- Use of staff to find data
- Development of proposals to respond to issues
- Development of alternative solutions
- Presentation and analysis of final proposal(s)
- Consensus and final resolution of the approach to be taken

Source: Adapted from recommendations by the U.S. Department of Transportation (2013).

Walker 2001; Innes and Booher 2000; Lewicki, Gray, and Elliott 2003). Through participation in crafting rules, those regulated and regulators learn more about each other's activities and become invested in solving a mutual problem. Consensus-building activities such as task forces, community boards, negotiated rule making, and charrettes (see Table 10.3) have been successfully used at many levels of government.

Managing Expectations

Innes and Booher (2000) note that public participation means different things to different people based on four conceptual models about how planning occurs, who should be involved, what information is relevant, and what the role of the public should be. Managing public expectation on their involvement level and quality is essential to deter miscommunication and build trust.

The bureaucratic model favors staff-generated technical reports with objective, scientific information that informs policy makers' decisions. Where there is little difference about overall goals or values, the bureaucratic model is efficient. In the bureaucratic model public involvement is a checkbox required by law.

The political influence model (also known as the pork barrel approach) solves problems based on the preferences of influential constituents. A project or rule can be dropped into legislation or rules created with scant public input. Public participation is seen as an undesirable complication. Public input may occur after the majority of major decisions have already been made.

Social movements may form when citizens feel excluded (or their preferred solutions do not prevail). Social movement participants feel like outsiders to the political process and attempt to influence policy via protests, lawsuits, and other strategies to slow the government process.

Collaborative processes are the newest model to reach the public stage. A variety of cooperative and inclusive techniques have been created. These processes engage stakeholders before decisions are made, educate citizens about the science and range of possible solutions, and help opposing parties participate in dialogue.

Expectations must be managed regardless of the type of process utilized. Publicity for an event and opening remarks at the beginning of a session should state the method available to the public for providing input. For example, appropriate means of response for the public might include asking questions at the end, writing questions to be asked by a moderator, or posting a comment on an electronic response board. Examples of inappropriate responses and consequences might include booing a speaker one disagrees with, interrupting, making long speeches when the format calls for short questions, and cursing or name calling.

A short speech about "democracy" and "democratic processes" or "the right of all audience members to hear the speaker they came to hear" might inoculate against some forms of creeping incivility. For example, at a debate on abortion rights between Sara Weddington (the attorney for Roe in the *Roe v. Wade* case) and Phyllis Schlaffley (conservative spokesperson against abortion), an audience of 1,200 heard a short speech about democratic processes, the right of each person in the audience to hear the people they came to hear, and a description of the event rules. Audience members were encouraged to applaud comments they liked and avoid outbursts. If outbursts persisted, they were told that time would be taken away from the speaker on their side. The first few people who hissed were quieted by those near them and the audience was loud and cheerful in applauding their favored side.

If the public is allowed to speak, expectations about the form of comments and length of time per person should be very clear. Is the forum open to any comment on any topic they choose? Can only questions be asked? At large events, it may be prudent to share the consequences of format rule violations. During the Weddington-Schlaffley debate, the audience was told they would have two minutes to form a question directed toward one of the speakers and that only questions would be allowed—no speeches. When the moderator didn't hear a question, she would speak over the top of the person and ask: "What is your question?" After listening for a few moments more and the "speech" continued, the moderator would say: "You have another 30 seconds to form your question and then we will cut you off." Individuals usually complied with the instructions. In fact, the audience sometimes was more vigilant than the moderator and would chant: "What's the question?" when someone started a speech.

The rules and description of the process must be sincere, consistently applied, and clear about what type of participation is appropriate on this particular occasion. In public sector work, information should be provided about other ways to state one's opinion on the topic (on the agency website or at other public meetings).

Tracy and Durfy (2007) studied school board meetings over time and discovered that inconsistent application of "rules" can themselves become points of contention or encourage incivility. They described one case in which rules seemed intended to discourage any form of disagreement with a board of directors.

> At the start of public participation, the board president would explain the . . . rules and then read a statement about the kind of communicative conduct that was expected. The exact statement varied slightly; below is one version.
>
> **Excerpt 1 (22 May 1997, line 34)**
>
> We are glad to hear from the public and we look forward to receiving your comments. The Board has unanimously resolved, however, that it cannot tolerate personal attacks upon Board members, administrators, teachers, or staff.
>
> ((murmurs from audience . . .)) We will also expect the audience to be extremely quiet during this discussion because this is actually an official board meeting and we need to conduct business. . . . We must all encourage and insist upon a more civil public discourse and we thank you for helping us to achieve that goal.
>
> Following the explanation of participation rules, speakers were called to the podium in groups of five. Each would take their presumably two-minute turn and sit down, and the president would call the names of the next five speakers. Participation rules were not straightforwardly followed. (p. 229)

Setting Rules for Speakers

Audience members are not the only ones who can foment incivility. Speakers at panels, debates, and public meetings must also agree to the rules and pledge to be civil. Time limits are an important element of rules. Inform speakers how they will be (politely) told their time is about to elapse or that it has elapsed. They also must be aware of the steps that will be taken if they go overtime or willfully subvert the agreed-upon process.

Using Microphones Strategically

In pure power terms, the person with the loudest microphone wins. Hopefully, that person is the moderator. If microphones are present for audience questions, it should be made possible for any one microphone to be turned off to silence extreme interruptions or those who go far beyond their allotted time. If handheld microphones are used during audience questions, choose assertive and strong people to hold the microphones during an audience member's comment and never let go.

Recording the Meeting

It seems that the more anonymous someone feels, the greater the likelihood of incivility. Announcing that a meeting is being recorded increases accountability. Likewise, asking people to state their name prior to making a comment may help.

Fostering Inclusion

People want to be heard. Sometimes, more people show up at a public participation meeting than can be accommodated during the scheduled time frame. In public sector work, it may be prudent to make arrangements for everyone to have their chance rather than to cut off those who are waiting their turn when the scheduled meeting time elapses. This may mean staying at a meeting for several hours. Alternately, meeting planners can provide computers where individuals can type their input comments onto a form. The written comments could be projected for a few minutes on a large screen during the meeting as well as collected for later review.

Choosing a Written Questions Format

A written-questions-only format does not allow the audience members to speak directly with the officials or speakers. The audience is given cards on which to write any questions. The cards are collected, then selected questions are posed to the speakers by the moderator. The moderator can pull out themes that run across several questions or reframe a question without using a writer's overly negative phrases. In this way, several participants hear their general interest area asked as a question, even though their exact words may not be used.

Diverting or Co-opting Gadflies

Some high energy citizens want to be involved, feel included, or be in the public eye at every meeting. Even frequent flyer gadflies deserve respect. Sometimes, high-energy participants can be invited to join committees or participate in research endeavors in an effort to harness their enthusiasm for the public good. Public meetings attract all sorts of people: gadflies, political wannabees, and CAVEs (citizens against virtually everything). The public input process in a democratic society means everyone has the privilege of stating their opinions (within the rules of the process) in an environment of respect.

Limitations

Every situation involving public input is different. When customizing the choices made for a specific event, keep in mind the following limitations.

Disagreement Is Different from Incivility

As members of the British Parliament can attest, being the "subject" of clever wit can be painful. However, a biting turn of phrase or blunt disagreement is not, by itself, incivility. Doubting an employee's competence is not incivility. Stating that one is hurt, mad, or experiencing some other affect is not, by itself, incivility. An excerpt from the Tracy and Durfy (2007) study illustrates a too thin-skinned response to disagreement:

Parent: I am *surprised* that school board members including one with a PhD in education would misunderstand ((audience applause)) the purpose of this test.

Pres: Just a moment, just a moment, no personal attacks please [that's] not appropriate. . . .

Parent: That's not personal. (p. 238)

Strategies such as negative rhetorical questions or the use of God and Devil terms (Tracy and Durfy 2007) are common ways to show disdain for public employees. Rhetorical questions imply a wrongdoing: "Will the decision be made when the public isn't around?" "When will you wake up to the dangers of these policies?" Citizens may argue for or against issues using code terms putting an evaluative slant on an issue or person. For example, the word "liberal" historically shifted meaning to become a Devil term (anything associated with the term is evil); supporting troops became a God term (anything associated with the term is good). Use of negative rhetorical questions or God and Devil terms do not automatically denote incivility.

Passion Can Be Civil or Uncivil

Speaking forcefully, waving ones arms around, using high volume, or showing emotion is not necessarily uncivil behavior. It is well documented that European Americans are less tolerant of emotional displays compared to other cultures. For example, a newcomer from an expressive culture may wave his arms around and virtually yell his comments at the panel during a public meeting. Learn to be accepting of forceful speaking styles.

Comments Can Be Civil but Inappropriate

Trent Lott's speech in praise of Strom Thurmond's active segregationist politics and racism did not cause his downfall because it was uncivil; it caused his downfall because it was wrong at that moment in history. Senator Lott's power and effectiveness diminished because his opinion was deemed socially out of step and inappropriate for a public servant. One response to the use of racial or other inappropriate comment is more speech by other citizens that exposes the derogatory language.

In contrast, hateful speech "aimed" a specific person may be the kind of incivility that requires a public official to intervene. For example, name-calling intended to hurt, demean, or silence a specific individual is inappropriate. Restricting speech content is always tricky business. Consult with superiors on how to respond to extreme incivility that may arise at public meetings.

Respect the Right to Be Arrested

Some protestors may arrive at a meeting expecting to be arrested. The tradition of civil disobedience sometimes includes attempts to disrupt governance. When protestors cannot be co-opted, ignored, worked around, or otherwise diverted from interfering with a public meeting process, removal by appropriate law enforcement authorities may be the only course of action. This delicate maneuver should be part of an agency's crisis management plan, along with how to remove drunk or deranged individuals. The strategy should be accomplished as gracefully and nonviolently as possible.

Civility Starts with the Leaders

If the person convening or moderating a meeting is not philosophically and strategically prepared to be civil, then little can be expected from the public. Meeting facilitators must either obtain the skills to maintain equilibrium under duress or pass the role of meeting management to someone who can. Likewise, the manner in which public officials treat each other makes a difference. The Institute for Local Government (2003) comments:

> [People who come to public meetings and complain or pontificate] are an intrinsic aspect of democracy, and there really is no "solution" to [them] except to try to understand what motivates them and appreciate the underlying democratic principle they represent. The worst strategy, of course, is to allow yourself to respond in kind to the type of angry, personal attacks gadflies are known to make. In addition to having your meetings sinking to the lowest common denominator, responding in kind also hands control over your behavior to others. (p. 11)

Case: Public Input to Locate the New Bypass

The county roads department is proposing a new bypass highway that will route traffic around Pineville, the county's largest city. The existing four-lane highway leads traffic through the center of the town in a meandering route that, while slow, guarantees access for visitors to downtown businesses. The county road department heralds the bypass as a solution to traffic flow. There are three alternatives for the location of the bypass. You have been given the task of organizing the public hearing process about the proposed three alternatives for the bypass location.

Discussion Questions

1. What formats do you think best in this situation?
2. How will you set up these hearings? Who should be invited?

11

The Interconnected Web
of People Skills

This book has offered insights from research and practical application for developing the skills to be an effective public manager. While there are many precise communication skills that could be formed into a comprehensive checklist for people skills, we feel it is more beneficial to view the endeavor of gaining competence within the arena of this book as a network of interconnectedness among skills, attitudes, and the choices about communication we make hundreds of times each day. Public sector employees come from a variety of places and have different degrees of communication skill. The recommendations in this book are guidelines that will be tempered by each individual's personality and style.

To guide our summative discussion of people skills for public sector leaders, we have selected ten points from the interconnected web of communication competencies. The ordinal ranking of these ten points is not relevant, as each point is inextricably tied to the overall web.

Nexus 1. Public Managers with People Skills
Demonstrate Resilience amid Change

The modern public sector organization paradoxically is caught between the weight of a ponderous bureaucracy and the turmoil of rapid change. Rarely does a public project survive from conception to implementation without the environment or circumstances changing—tax revenues rise and fall with the general economy, public opinion and political directives dart hither and yon, private sector partners emerge and disappear, or the science and technology driving a project abruptly changes. Resilience requires the emotional and intellectual will to move forward toward a goal while the details swirl and change. Those who are not open to adaptation, who view flexibility as a weakness, or who are so self-involved they do not see serendipitous opportunity when it presents itself are less competent public managers. Resilient public managers are prepared to make a one-minute pitch about a partnership opportunity when chance places them in an elevator with a CEO. Those who are resilient have the ability to scan their environment and ask analytical questions to prepare for change. They overcome communication barriers by adapting their communication style to the styles of others and learning about the styles of diverse populations.

Nexus 2. Public Managers with People Skills Are Able to Separate Listening from Analyzing

Real listening is an intensive activity. Good listeners have the emotional intelligence to seek understanding instead of becoming defensive. Superior listeners check their perceptions before moving on to analyze or respond to others' comments instead of leaping into the abyss of false assumptions. Quality listening is a whole-body, focused attention experience—taking in nonverbal and verbal messages, assessing them in context, and discerning what is important. Listeners bring the appropriate skills to the table for each changing interaction.

This book presented several listening skills, including the ability to ask curious questions and validate others' emotions as an efficiency technique. Numerous other listening skills exist that can be added to one's list for future development.

Nexus 3. Public Managers with People Skills Understand the Interests of Others

Every behavior of someone else that seems odd makes good sense—to that person. Misunderstanding occurs because the recipient of someone else's good sense doesn't have the appropriate code book to understand the message. Wanting to understand others is an attitude that facilitates the accomplishment of public work. Skills such as cultural awareness, mapping of interests, and understanding how motivation may vary across generations facilitate better conversations and more advantageous negotiations. Competent public managers learn more about themselves and their root cultures as a step toward understanding others, relate to diversity, and enable the synergy that can occur when difference is harnessed in the service of creativity. When the overlapping interest among stakeholders is found, leverage toward problem solving is created.

There is an undervalued interest among subordinates, volunteers, and sometimes even the general public—the desire to feel connected with leaders. Remembering a subordinate's or member of the public's name, visiting field offices, creating listening sessions, praising volunteers, or even participating in staff picnics allow others to feel a bond with their leaders. A savvy leader will agree to play a part in a silly skit at an annual recognition event (assuming it is in good taste and not offensive) rather than remain aloof.

Nexus 4. Public Managers with People Skills Prefer Collaboration, But Are Able to Make Quick Decisions

One criticism from a city manager with a business background was that MPA graduates overanalyze everything. Competent public managers can discern when an issue's immediacy and size requires an immediate response and when stakeholders should be involved. When time allows, the most competent public managers prefer to include others—even when stakeholder inclusion is not required by statute. Involving others may increase stakeholder buy-in and decrease knee-jerk opposition to surprises. Competent public managers want to engage in conversation with those who disagree to search for common ground, or at least convey that every effort was made to understand others' interests. These managers prefer nonadversarial processes and refuse to frame issues in win-lose terms. Competent public managers continuously scan the environment for potential partners and emerging stakeholder groups. The old adage that "it is lonely at the top" no longer applies. Leaders need a broad network of connections and an array of trusted advisors for confidential strategizing about emerging issues. Leaders know they can't collaborate their way out of every problem. Even though collaboration is preferred, competent communicators are prepared for hard-nosed traditional negotiation when it is required—while at the same time trying to persuade intransigent competitors that their own interests might be better served through collaboration.

Nexus 5. Public Managers with People Skills Build Relationships

The move from an entry-level position to upper management means shifting focus from discrete tasks to people and processes. In a very real sense, efficiency is born in relationships. Those who feel they have good working relationships with their leaders are more likely get things done quickly and easily.

Building relationships engages a variety of interpersonal skills. Those who work to become emotionally intelligent will find relationship development easier. Coworkers, subordinates, and the public need not become the public employee's friends, but should feel there is enough of a positive relationship so collaboration can occur when it is appropriate.

Nexus 6. Public Managers with People Skills Are Accountable

Public leaders must set high expectations for their personal behaviors and the behaviors of those with whom they interact. Any perception of misuse of the public trust stains everyone who works in public service. Leaders are accountable for the communicative systems in which they interact and cannot ignore ethical lapses that are observed in those who work for them. Competent public managers understand the reputational risk of ignoring ethics, creating lax environments in which individual employees interact in unrestrained ways with the public, or letting misperceptions fester.

Having an awareness of personal boundaries and ethics is important. Any communication-competent leader will adhere to a professional code of conduct. Accountability means much more for public sector leaders. Accountability includes simple choices such as only making promises you are able to keep. It also means more profound behaviors such as communicating in a civil way with thoughtfully chosen words when confronted by those with whom one disagrees. To that end, public leaders are accountable for creating positive, future-oriented atmospheres rather than climates where others feel free to revel in negative invective, bullying, or agency-damaging labeling ("I'd like to help, but the director is just an imbecile"). By choosing accountability, a public leader accepts that actions and the reasoning behind them must be transparent and that confidentiality should be kept (if the information is not obligated to be disclosed by statute). Communicative accountability means taking responsibility for one's share of misunderstandings and learning to frame comments in ways that avoid provoking defensiveness in others. Accountability means the public leader sets clear expectations and reasonable goals, and has the wherewithal to hold others accountable as well.

Nexus 7. Public Managers with People Skills Communicate Effectively

It may seem obvious from the discussion in the first six nexus points that communication is at the heart of people skills. Communication effectiveness, however, involves how a public leader thinks, what criteria are used to analyze others' messages, how diverse people are perceived, and a vast array of specific verbal and nonverbal tools. Effective communication is situational and personal—what is effective in one conversation may be inappropriate in the next. Effective communicators discern which skills are appropriate and then apply those skills competently.

Public managers should become adept at listening, speaking, developing relationships, managing meetings, responding to conflict, being persuasive, advocating vigorously, leading others through problem solving, and other communication skills appropriate to their specific situations. Developing emotional intelligence so one can decode feedback during a conversation is important—to detect the subtle nonverbal messages that indicate agreement, disagreement, or confusion. Competent communicators develop multiple strategies to convey messages clearly, can overcome communicative style differences, and hone the ability to moderate others' emotions when they interfere with goal achievement.

Nexus 8. Public Managers with People Skills Share Power

Traditional views might suggest someone with positional authority can make decisions and give instructions that everyone else must obey. Contemporary leaders recognize that forcing people to comply is a perilous strategy. Sharing power does not mean ceding any of one's statutory obligations as much as it describes the processes through which tasks are accomplished and obligations met. The predisposition to include others in problem analysis, idea generation, or goal setting demonstrates the sharing of power with stakeholders and employees. The ability to lead others through a problem-solving process is a skill worth developing.

Public leaders competent at people skills are comfortable with their own power—neither needing to hold it tightly as a cherished personal possession nor to wield it like a club to force others into submission. Sharing power allows creativity and outside-the-box thinking. Those competent at sharing power are comfortable with personal strengths and limitations and surround themselves with others who complement their skills.

Nexus 9. Public Managers with People Skills Are Persistent

In the public sector, moving toward an agency's goal can be a circuitous process. Budget levels come and go. Staff levels and abilities rise and fall. Community partners—particularly from the private sector—pop up in unexpected ways and may disappear with the bursting of an economic bubble. While the overarching agency goal remains the same, many other variables may change. Moving toward a goal requires persistence over time. Likewise, changing an employee's substandard behavior (or moving toward termination) can be a long process, more like a campaign than a series of discrete actions. A supervisor may have multiple conversations with an employee so the employee understands what is expected, set short-term goals, coach, monitor, assess, and then repeat the process until the employee reaches a level of adequate performance or steps are taken toward termination. Improving employee performance or moving toward agency goals requires persistent vigilance instead of occasional, offhand attention.

Nexus 10. Public Managers with People Skills Embrace Continuous Improvement

Competence is not gauged by mastery of any one specific communication action—it arises from numerous skills guided by an attitude of respect for those with whom we work. The acquisition of communication skill, knowledge of cultures, and comfort with diversity are lifelong enterprises. At each stage in a career, self-awareness can increase, current skills may deepen, and new communication techniques are learned. Public managers should continuously work toward short-term communication improvement goals. When one goal is accomplished, move on to the next. As a senior city clerk in a western U.S. city commented, "You can never stop learning."

Bibliography

Abel, C. F. 2009. "Toward a Signature Pedagogy for Public Administration." *Journal of Public Affairs Education* 15, no. 2: 145–160.

Adubato, Steve. 2009. "Don't Be a Communication Casualty." Blog post, August 17. http://blog.nj.com/steveadubato/2009/08/dont_be_a_communication_casual. html.

Ashkanasy, Neal M., Wilfred J. Zerbe, and Charmine E. J. Hartel. 2002. "Managing Emotions in a Changing Workplace." In *Managing Emotions in the Workplace,* ed. Neal. M. Ashkanasy, Wilfred J. Zerbe, and Charmine E. J. Hartel, 3–24. Armonk, NY: M.E. Sharpe.

Atwater, Leanne E., Joan F. Brett, and Atira Cherise Charles. 2007. "The Delivery of Workplace Discipline: Lessons Learned." *Organizational Dynamics* 36, no. 4: 392–403.

Ayoko, Oluremi B., Victor J. Callan, and Charmine E. J. Hartel. 2003. "Workplace Conflict, Bullying, and Counterproductive Behaviors." *International Journal of Organizational Analysis* 11, no. 4: 283–301.

Babcock-Roberson, Meredith Elaine, and Oriel J. Strickland. 2010. "The Relationship between Charismatic Leadership, Work Engagement, and Organizational Citizenship Behaviors." *Journal of Psychology* 144, no. 3: 313–326.

Baron, Robert A., and Joel H. Neuman. 1996. "Workplace Violence and Workplace Aggression: Evidence on Their Relative Frequency and Potential Causes." *Aggressive Behavior* 22, no. 3: 161–173.

———. 1998. "Workplace Aggression—The Iceberg Beneath the Tip of Workplace Violence: Evidence on Its Forms, Frequency, and Targets." *Public Affairs Quarterly* 21, no. 4: 446–464.

Bartholome, Paula T. 2003. "The Civility of Listening." *Listening Professional* 2, no. 1: 9–12.

Bartlett, James E., and Michelle E. Bartlett. 2011. "Workplace Bullying: An Integrative Literature Review." *Advances in Developing Human Resources* 13, no. 1: 69–84.

Berman, Evan M. and Jonathan P. West. 2008. "Managing Emotional Intelligence in U.S. Cities: A Study of Social Skills among Public Managers." *Public Administration Review* 68, no. 4: 742–758.

Bible, Jon D. 2012. "The Jerk At Work: Workplace Bullying and the Law's Inability to Combat It." *Employee Relations Law Journal* 38, no. 1: 32–51.

Bill 168. 2009. An Act to Amend the Occupational Health and Safety Act with Respect to Violence and Harassment in the Workplace and Other Matters. April 20. 1st Session, 39th Legislature, Ontario, Canada.

Borrego, Espiridion, and Richard Greggory Johnson. 2012. *Cultural Competence for Public Managers.* Boca Raton, FL: CRC Press.

Breaux, Denise M., Pamela L. Perrewe, Angela T. Hall, Dwight D. Frink, and Wayne A. Hochwarter. 2008. "Time to Try a Little Tenderness? The Detrimental Effects of Accountability When Coupled with Abusive Supervision." *Journal of Leadership & Organizational Studies* 15, no. 2: 111–122.

Brehm, John, and Scott Gates. 1997. *Working, Shirking, and Sabotage: Bureaucratic Response to a Democratic Public.* Ann Arbor: University of Michigan Press.

Bright, Leonard. 2008. "Does Public Service Motivation Really Make a Difference on the Job Satisfaction and Turnover Intentions of Public Employees?" *American Review of Public Administration* 38, no. 2: 149–166.

Buelens, Marc, and Herman Van den Broeck. 2007. "An Analysis of Differences in Work Motivation between Public and Private Sector Organizations." *Public Administration Review* 67, no. 1: 65–74.

Cai, Deborah A., and Edward L. Fink. 2002. "Conflict Style Differences between Individualists and Collectivists." *Communication Monographs* 69, no. 1: 67–87.

Calabrese, Kirk R. 2000. "Interpersonal Conflict and Sarcasm in the Workplace." *Genetic, Social, and General Psychology Monographs* 126, no. 4: 459–494.

Campbell, David. 2004. "Nine Keys to Good Leadership." In *The CCL Guide to Leadership in Action: How Managers and Organizations Can Improve the Practice of Leadership*, ed. Martin Wilcox and Stephen Rush, 29–33. San Francisco: Jossey-Bass.

Carnevale, David G., and Kay Ham. 2010. "Going Beyond Human Resource Management Technique." In *Handbook of Human Resource Management in Government*, ed. Stephen E. Condrey, 261–277. San Francisco: Jossey-Bass.

Carrizales, Tony. 2010. "Exploring Cultural Competency within the Public Affairs Curriculum." *Journal of Public Affairs Education* 16, no. 4: 593–606.

Chappelow, Craig, and Jean Brittain Leslie. 2004. "Throwing the Right Switches: How to Keep Your Executive Career on Track." In *The CCL Guide to Leadership in Action: How Managers and Organizations Can Improve the Practice of Leadership*, ed. Martin Wilcox and Stephen Rush, 125–134. San Francisco: Jossey-Bass.

Chiu, Chia-Yen, Lin Hao-Chieh, and Shu-Hwa Chien. 2009. "Transformational Leadership and Team Behavior Integration: The Mediating Role of Team Learning." *Academy of Management Proceedings*: 1–6.

Chory, Rebecca M., and Catherine Y. Kingsley Westerman. 2009. "Feedback and Fairness: The Relationship between Negative Performance Feedback and Organizational Justice." *Western Journal of Communication* 73, no. 2: 157–181.

Cianci, Anna M., Howard J. Klein, and Gerald H. Seijts. 2010. "The Effect of Negative Feedback on Tension and Subsequent Performance: The Main and Interactive Effects of Goal Content and Conscientiousness." *Journal of Applied Psychology* 95, no. 4: 618–630.

Cloven, Denise H., and Michael E. Roloff. 1991. "Sense-Making Activities and Interpersonal Conflict: Communicative Cures for the Mulling Blues." *Western Journal of Communication* 55, no. 2: 134–158.

Cole, Nina D. 2008a. "Consistency in Employee Discipline: An Empirical Exploration." *Personnel Review* 37, no. 1: 109–117.

———. 2008b. "The Effects of Differences in Explanations, Employee Attributions, Type of Infraction, and Discipline Severity on Perceived Fairness of Employee Discipline." *Canadian Journal of Administrative Sciences* 25, no. 2: 107–120.

The Conflict Resolution Network. 2008. Conflict Resolution Trainers Manual, 2d ed. http://www.crnhq.org/pages.php?pID=7.

Coombs, W. T., and Sherry J. Holladay. 2004. "Understanding the Aggressive Workplace: Development of the Workplace Aggression Tolerance Questionnaire." *Communication Studies* 55, no. 3: 481–497.

Cowan, Renee L. 2011. "'Yes, We Have an Anti-Bullying Policy, But . . .:' HR Professionals' Understanding and Experiences with Workplace Bullying Policy." *Communication Studies* 62, no. 3: 307–327.

Cowan, Renee L. 2012. "It's Complicated: Defining Workplace Bullying from the Human Resource Professional's Perspective." *Management Communication Quarterly* 26, no. 3: 377–403.

Crewson, Philip E. 1997. "Public-Service Motivation: Building Empirical Evidence of Incidence and Effect." *Journal of Public Administration Research and Theory* 7, no. 4: 499–518.

Daley, Dennis M. 2007. "If a Tree Falls in the Forest: The Effect of Grievances on Employee Perceptions of Performance Appraisal, Efficacy, and Job Satisfaction." *Review of Public Policy Personnel Administration* 27, no. 3: 281–296.

———. 2008. "The Burden of Dealing with Poor Performers: Wear and Tear on Supervisory Organizational Engagement." *Review of Public Personnel Administration* 28, no. 1: 44–59.

Daniels, Steven E., and Gregg B. Walker. 2001. *Working Through Environmental Conflict: The Collaborative Learning Approach.* Westport, CT: Praeger.

Dierickx, Constance. 2004. "The Bully Employee: A Survival Guide for Supervisors." *Supervision* 65, no. 3: 7–12.

Dreeke, Robin K., and Joe Navarro. 2009. "Behavioral Mirroring in Interviewing." *FBI Law Enforcement Bulletin* (December): 1–10.

Eddy, Bill. 2011. "Dealing with Defensiveness in High Conflict People." Mediate. com, November. www.mediate.com/articles/eddyB6.cfm.

Emerson, Richard M. 1962. "Power-Dependence Relations." *American Sociological Review* 27: 31–41.

Estes, Brad, and Jia Wang. 2008. "Workplace Incivility: Impacts on Individual and Organizational Performance." *Human Resource Development Review* 7, no. 2: 218–240.

Farmer, Steven, and Anson Seers. 2004. "Time Enough to Work: Employee Motivation and Entrainment in the Workplace." *Time & Society* 13, nos. 2/3: 265–284.

Felps, Will, Terence R. Michell, and Eliza Byington. 2006. "How, When, and Why Bad Apples Spoil the Barrel: Negative Group Members and Dysfunctional Groups." *Research in Organizational Behavior* 27: 175–222.

Fernandez, Sergio, and Tina Moldogazie. 2011. "Empowering Public Sector Employees to Improve Performance: Does It Work?" *American Review of Public Administration* 41, no. 1: 23–47.

Field, Tim. 1996. *Bully in Sight: How To Predict, Resist, Challenge and Combat Workplace Bullying.* Oxfordshire, UK: Wessex Press.

Fletcher, Beverly R., & Cooke, Alfred. L. 2012. "Self-Awareness and Leadership Success." In *The Trusted Leader: Building Relationships that Make Government Work,* ed. Terry Newell, Grant Reeher, and Peter Ronayne, 2d ed., 53–81. Los Angeles: Sage.

Frank, Sue A., and Gregory B. Lewis. 2004. "Government Employees: Working

Hard or Hardly Working?" *American Review of Public Administration* 34: 36–51.

Frederickson, H. George, and Kevin B. Smith. 2003. *The Public Administration Theory Primer.* Boulder, CO: Westview.

French, John P., and Bertram Raven. 1959. "The Bases of Social Power." In *Studies in Social Power,* ed. D. Cartwright, 86–91. Ann Arbor, MI: Institution for Social Research.

Friedman, Raymond A., and Steven C. Currall. 2003. "Conflict Escalation: Dispute Exacerbating Elements of E-Mail Communication." *Human Relations* 56, no. 11: 1325–1347.

Funder, David C. 2001."The Really, Really Fundamental Attribution Error." *Psychological Inquiry* 12, no. 1: 21–23.

Funke, Gail. 2012. "Leading for Team Success." In *The Trusted Leader: Building Relationships that Make Government Work,* ed. Terry Newell, Grant Reeher, and Peter Ronayne, 2d ed., 137–169. Los Angeles: Sage.

Geddes, Deanna, and Lisa T. Stickney. 2010. "The Trouble with Sanctions: Organizational Responses to Deviant Anger Displays at Work." *Human Relations* 64, no. 2: 201–230.

Gibb, James. 1961. "Defensive Communication." *Journal of Communication* 11: 141–168.

Giegold, William C., and Richard J. Dunsing. 1978. "Team-Building in the Local Jurisdiction: Two Case Studies." *Public Administration Review* 38, no. 1: 59–63.

Glassman, Myron, Aaron Glassman, Paul J. Champagne, and Michael T. Zugelder. 2010. "Evaluating Pay-for-Performance Systems: Critical Issues for Implementation." *Compensation & Benefits Review* 42, no. 4: 231–238.

Glendinning, Peter M. 2001. "Workplace Bullying: Curing the Cancer of the American Workplace." *Public Personnel Management* 30, no. 3: 269–287.

Goldsmith, Stephen, and Robert D. Eggers. 2004. *Governing by Network: The New Shape of the Public Sector.* Washington, DC: Brookings Institution Press.

Goleman, Daniel, and Richard Boyatzis. 2008. "Social Intelligence and the Biology of Leadership." *Harvard Business Review* 86, no. 9: 74–81.

Gordon, Tom, Allison Linney, Kristina Energia Naranjo-Rivera, and Michael Rawlings. 2012. "The Diversity Opportunity." In *The Trusted Leader: Building Relationships That Make Government Work,* ed. Terry Newell, Grant Reeher, and Peter Ronayne, 2d ed., 201–238. Los Angeles: Sage.

Grandey, Alicia A., and Jennifer A. Diamond. 2010. "Interactions with the Public: Bridging Job Design and Emotional Labor Perspectives." *Journal of Organizational Behavior* 31: 338–350.

Guy, Mary E., and Meredith A. Newman. 2010. "Valuing Diversity in the Changing Workplace." In *Handbook of Human Resource Management in Government,* ed. Stephen E. Condrey, 149–169. San Francisco: Jossey-Bass.

Halachmi, Ari, and Theo van der Krogt. 2010. "Motivating Employees: The Role of the Manager." In *Handbook of Human Resource Management in Government,* ed. Stephen E. Condrey, 519–554. San Francisco: Jossey-Bass.

Hall, Edward T. 1976. *Beyond Culture.* Garden City, NY: Anchor.

Hammer, Mitchell R. 2002. *Resolving Conflict Across the Cultural Divide: Differences in Intercultural Conflict Styles.* Minneapolis, MN: Hammer Consulting.

———. 2005. "The Intercultural Conflict Style Inventory: A Conceptual Framework and Measure of Intercultural Conflict Resolution Approaches." *International Journal of Intercultural Relations* 29: 675–695.

Hartman, Jackie L., and Jim McCambridge. 2011. "Optimizing Millennials' Communication Styles." *Business Communication Quarterly* 74: 22–44.

Harvey, Michael Darren Treadway, Joyce Tompson Heames, and Allison Duke. 2009. "Bullying in the 21st Century Global Organization: An Ethical Perspective." *Journal of Business Ethics* 85: 27–40.

Hays, Steven W., and Jessica E. Sowa. 2010. "Staffing the Bureaucracy: Employee Recruitment and Selection." *Handbook of Human Resource Management in Government,* ed. Stephen E. Condrey, 99–128. San Francisco: Jossey-Bass.

Heifetz, Ronald A., and Donald L. Laurie. 1997. "The Work of Leadership." *Harvard Business Review* 75, no. 1: 124–134.

The Hofstede Center. 2013. "National Cultural Dimensions." http://geert-hofstede.com/national-culture.html.

Hughes, Marcia L., Bonita Patterson, and James Bradford Terrell. 2005. *Emotional Intelligence in Action.* San Francisco: Pfeiffer.

Hughes, Marcia, and James Bradford Terrell. 2007. *The Emotionally Intelligent Team.* San Francisco: Jossey-Bass.

Innes, Judith E., and David E. Booher. 2000. "Public Participation in Planning: New Strategies for the 21st Century." Institute of Urban and Regional Development Working Paper Series: WP 2000'07.

Institute for Local Government. 2003. *Promoting Civility at Public Meetings: Concepts and Practice.* August, October. Sacramento, CA: ILG.

Jandt, Fred E. 2012. *An Introduction to Intercultural Communication: Identities in a Global Community.* San Francisco: Sage.

Johnson, Danette Ifert, and Nicole Lewis. 2010. "Perception of Swearing in the Work Setting: An Expectancy Violations Theory Perspective." *Communication Reports* 23, no. 1: 106–118.

Jones, John E. 2003. "Dealing with Disruptive People in Meetings." In *Pfeiffer's Classic Activities for Managing Conflict at Work,* ed. Jack Gordon, 75–80. San Francisco: John Wiley & Sons.

Kanaga, Kim, and Sonya Prestridge. 2004. "The Right Start: A Team's First Meeting Is Key. " In *The CCL Guide to Leadership in Action*, ed. Martin Wilcox and Stephen Rush, 243–251. San Francisco: Jossey-Bass.

Kassing, Jeffrey W., and Theodore A. Avtgis. 1999. "Examining the Relationship between Organizational Dissent and Aggressive Communication." *Management Communication Quarterly* 13, no. 1: 100–115.

Keashly, Loraleigh, and Karen Jagatic. 2003. "By Any Other Name: American Perspectives on Workplace Bullying." In *Bullying and Emotional Abuse in the Workplace*, ed. Stale Einarsen, Helge Hoel, Dieter Zapf, and Cary L. Cooper, 31–61. London: Taylor & Francis.

Kennedy, George A. 1991. *Aristotle on Rhetoric: A Theory of Civic Discourse.* New York: Oxford University Press.

Kim, Seok Eun, and Jung Wook Lee. 2007. "Is Mission Attachment an Effective Management Tool for Employee Retention: An Empirical Analysis of a Nonprofit Human Services Agency." *Review of Public Personnel Administration* 27, no. 3: 227–248.

Klein, Cameron, Deborah Diaz Granados, Eduardo Salas, Huy Le, C. Shawn Burke, Rebecca Lyons, and Gerald F. Goodwin. 2009. "Does Team Building Work?" *Small Group Research* 40, no. 2: 181–222.

Koenig, Seth. 2011. "Brennan to Become Portland's First Popularly Elected Mayor in 88 Years." *Bangor Daily News*, November 9.

Kohut, Margaret R. 2008. *The Complete Guide to Understanding, Controlling, and Stopping Bullies and Bullying at Work.* Ocala, FL: Atlantic.

Kuhn, Tim, and Marshall Scott Poole. 2000. "Do Conflict Management Styles Affect Group Decision Making?" *Human Communication Research* 26, no. 4: 558–590.

Lan, Zhiyong. 1997. "A Conflict Resolution Approach to Public Administration." *Public Administration Review* 57, no. 1: 27–35.

LaVan, Helen, Marsha Katz, and Michael Jay Jedel. 2010, February. "The Public Sector Manager as a Bully: Analysis of Litigated Cases." *Proceedings of the ASBBS Annual Conference.* Las Vegas.

Leck, Joanne D., and Bella L. Galperin. 2006. "Worker Responses to Bully Bosses." *Canadian Public Policy* 32, no. 1: 85–97.

Lewicki, Roy, Barbara Gray, and Michael Elliott, eds. 2003. *Making Sense of Intractable Environmental Conflicts: Concepts and Cases.* Washington, DC: Island Press.

Linden, Russ. 2012. "Collaborating Across Organizational Boundaries." In *The Trusted Leader: Building Relationships That Make Government Work,* ed. Terry Newell, Grant Reeher, and Peter Ronayne, 2d ed., 239–264. Los Angeles: Sage.

Lizzio, Alf, Keitha Wilson, and Lori MacKay. 2008. "Managers' and Subordinates' Evaluations of Feedback Strategies: The Critical Contribution of Voice." *Journal of Applied Social Psychology* 38, no. 4: 919–946.

Lutgen-Sandvik, Pamela. 2003. "The Communicative Cycle of Employee Emotional Abuse: Generation and Regeneration of Workplace Mistreatment." *Management Communication Quarterly* 16, no. 4: 471–501.

Lutgen-Sandvik, Pamela, and Virginia McDermott. 2011. "Making Sense of Supervisory Bullying: Perceived Powerlessness, Empowered Possibilities." *Southern Communication Journal* 76, no. 4: 342–368.

Lutgen-Sandvik, Pamela, and Sarah J. Tracy. 2011. "Answering Five Key Questions About Workplace Bullying: How Communication Scholarship Provides Thought Leadership for Transforming Abuse at Work." *Management Communication Quarterly* 26, no. 1: 3–47.

Macey, William H., Benjamin Schneider, Karen M. Barbera, and Scott A. Young. 2009. *Employee Engagement.* Malden, MA: Wiley-Blackwell.

MacIntosh, Judith. 2006. "Tackling Work Place Bullying." *Issues in Mental Health Nursing* 27: 665–679.

Madlock, Paul E., and Megan R. Dillow. 2012. "The Consequences of Verbal Aggression in the Workplace: An Application of the Investment Model." *Communication Studies* 63, no. 5: 593–607.

Madlock, Paul E., and Carrie Kennedy-Lightsey. 2010. "The Effects of Supervisors' Verbal Aggressiveness and Mentoring on Their Subordinates." *Journal of Business Communication* 47, no. 1: 42–62.

Markle, Garold L. 2010. "The Weakness Trap." *EHS Today.* April 6. http://ehstoday. com/safety/management/weakness-trap-0321.

Masters, Marick F., and Robert R. Albright. 2002. *The Complete Guide to Conflict Resolution in the Workplace.* New York: American Management Association.

Mayfield, Jacqueline, and Milton Mayfield. 2009. "The Role of Leader Motivating Language in Employee Absenteeism." *Journal of Business Communication* 46, no. 4: 455–479.

McCorkle, Suzanne, and Melanie J. Reese. 2010. *Personal Conflict Management.* Boston: Allyn & Bacon.

Miles, Rufus E. 1978. "The Origin and Meaning of Miles' Law." *Public Administration Review* 38, no. 5: 399–403.

Mutz, Diana C., and Byron Reeves. 2005. "The New Videomalaise: Effects of Televised Incivility on Political Trust." *American Political Science Review* 99, no. 1: 1–15.

Namie, Gary M. 2003. *The WBTI 2003 Report on Abusive Workplaces.* The Workplace Bullying and Trauma Institute.

Newman, Meredith A., Mary E. Guy, and Sharon H. Mastracci. 2009. "Beyond Cognition: Affective Leadership and Emotional Labor." *Public Administration Review* 69, no. 1: 6–20.

Nielsen, Morten Birkeland, and Ståle Einarsen. 2012. "Outcomes of Exposures to Workplace Bullying: A Meta-Analytic Review." *Work and Stress* 26, no. 4: 309–332.

Nkomo, Stella M. 2010. "Social Identity: Understanding the In-Group/Out-Group Phenomenon." In *Leading Across Differences: Cases and Perspectives*, ed. Kelly M. Hannum, Belinda B. McFeeters, and Lize Booysen, 73–79. San Francisco: John Wiley.

Noonan, William R. 2007. *Discussing the Undiscussable: A Guide to Overcoming Defensive Routines in the Workplace.* San Francisco: John Wiley.

Norman-Major, Kristina A., and Susan T. Gooden. 2012. *Cultural Competency for Public Administrators.* Armonk, NY: M.E. Sharpe.

Office of Personnel Management, 2012. "Senior Executive Service Executive Core Qualifications." http://www.opm.gov/policy-data-oversight/senior-executive-service/executive-core-qualifications/.

Olson-Buchanan, Julie B., and W. R. Boswell. 2009. *Mistreatment in the Workplace: Prevention and Resolution for Managers and Organizations.* West Sussex, UK: Wiley-Blackwell.

Omari, Maryam. 2007. Towards Dignity and Respect at Work: An Exploration of Bullying in the Public Sector. Ph.D. diss., Edith Cowan University.

Pandey, Sanjay K. 2010. "Cutback Management and the Paradox of Publicness." *Public Administration Review* 70, no. 4: 564–571.

Pandey, Sanjay K., and James L. Garnett. 2006. "Exploring Public Sector Communication Performance: Testing a Model and Drawing Implications." *Public Administration Review* 66, no. 1: 37–51.

Peroff, Nicolas C. 2011, April. "Rethinking Tribal Leadership: Traditional Worldviews and Managing Complexity in the 21st Century." Paper presented at the Western Social Science Association Meeting. Salt Lake City, Utah.

Perry, James L., Debra Mesch, and Laurie Paarlberg. 2006. "Motivating Employees in a New Governance Era: The Performance Paradigm Revisited." *Public Administration Review* 66, no. 4: 505–514.

The Pew Research Center. 2010. *Distrust, Discontent, Anger and Partisan Rancor: The People and Their Government.* Washington, DC: The Pew Research Center. www.people-press.org/2010/04/18/distrust-discontent-anger-and-partisan-rancor/.

Poindexter, Kate. 2008. "Passing the Torch: But Not Just Yet." *Public Manager* (Summer): 11–14.

Porath, Christine, and Christine Pearson. 2009. "How Toxic Colleagues Corrode Performance." *Harvard Business Review* (April): 24.

Prince, Don W., and Michael H. Hoppe. 2004. "Getting the Message: How to Feel Your Way With Other Cultures." In the *CCL Guide to Leadership in Action: How Managers and Organizations Can Improve the Practice of Leadership*, ed. Martin Wilcox and Stephen Rush, 73–82. San Francisco: Jossey-Bass.

Prindeville, Diane-Michele, and Carrie D. La Tour. 2012. "Cultural Diplomacy: Collaborations between Tribal and State Governments." In *Cultural Competency for Public Administrators,* ed. Kristina A. Norman-Major and Susan T. Gooden, 121–140. Armonk, NY: M.E. Sharpe.

Pryor, Mildred Golden, Lisa Pryor Singleton, Sonia Taneja, and Leslie A. Toombs. 2009. "Teaming as a Strategic and Tactical Tool: An Analysis with Recommendations." *International Journal of Management* 26, no. 2: 320–333.

Raines, Claire, and Jim Hunt. 2000. *The Xers and the Boomers: From Adversaries to Allies.* Menlo Park, CA: Crisp Publications.

Randall, Peter. 1997. *Adult Bullying: Perpetrators and Victims.* London: Routledge.

Reinhardt, Kari. 2004. "The Ugly Employee." *BC Business* 32: 4.

Reynolds, Garr. 2008. *Presentation Zen: Simple Ideas on Presentation Design and Delivery.* Berkeley, CA: New Riders Publications.

Riccucci, Norma. 2002. *Managing Diversity in Public Sector Workforces.* Boulder, CO: Westview.

Rice, Mitchell F. 2007. "A Post-Modern Cultural Competency Framework for Public Administration and Public Service Delivery." *International Journal of Public Sector Management* 20, no. 7: 622–637.

Rittel, Horst W. J., and Melvin M. Webber. 1973. "Dilemmas in a General Theory of Planning." *Policy Sciences* 4: 155–169.

Rivera, Mario A., Greggory Johnson, and James D. Ward. 2010. "The Ethics of Pedagogical Innovation in Diversity and Cultural Competency Education." *Innovation Journal* 15, no. 2: 1–20.

Robert, Henry Martyn. Robert's Rules of Order. 1876. http://www.constitution.org/rror/rror-01.htm.

Ruderman, Marian N., and Donna Chrobot-Mason. 2010. "Triggers of Social Identity Conflict." In *Leading across Differences: Cases and Perspectives*, ed. Kelly M. Hannum, Belinda B. McFeeters, and Lize Booysen, 81–94. San Francisco: John Wiley & Sons.

Ruderman, Marian N., Kelly Hannum, Jean Brittain Leslie, and Judith L. Steed. 2004. "Making the Connection: Leadership Skills and Emotional Intelligence." In *The CCL Guide to Leadership in Action: How Managers and Organizations Can Improve the Practice of Leadership,* ed. Martin Wilcox and Stephen Rush, 3–14. San Francisco: Jossey-Bass.

Ruell, E., N. Burkardt, and D. R. Clark. 2010. "Resolving Disputes over Science in Natural Resource Agency Decisionmaking." *Technical Memorandum* 86-68211-10-01. Denver, CO: U.S. Bureau of Reclamation.

Rush, Stephen. 2004. "Redefining Accountability: A Talk with Peter Block." In *The CCL Guide to Leadership in Action: How Managers and Organizations*

Can Improve the Practice of Leadership, ed. Martin Wilcox and Stephen Rush, 22–29. San Francisco: Jossey-Bass.

Sachs, Steven M. 2011. "Remembering the Traditional Meaning and Role of Kinship in American Indian Societies to Overcome Problems of Favoritism in Contemporary Tribal Government." *Indigenous Policy Journal* 22, no. 2: 1–12.

Salamon, M. Lester. 2002. *The Tools of Government: A Guide to the New Governance.* Oxford: Oxford University Press.

Sanders, Donald E., Patricia Pattison, and Jon D. Bible. 2012. "Legislating 'Nice': Analysis and Assessment of Proposed Workplace Bullying Prohibitions." *Southern Law Journal* 22, no. 1: 1–36.

Sandman, Peter M. 2008. "Meeting Management: Where Does Risk Communication Fit in Public Participation?" March 19. www.psandman.com/col/meeting.htm.

Shannon, Candice A., Kathleen M. Rospenda, and Judith A. Richman. 2007. "Workplace Harassment Patterning, Gender, and Utilization of Professional Services: Findings from a US National Study." *Social Science and Medicine* 64, no. 7: 1178–1191.

Sims, David. 2005. "You Bastard: A Narrative Exploration of the Experience of Indignation within Organizations." *Organization Studies* 26, no. 11: 1625–1640.

Society for Human Resource Management. 2008. "Selected Cross-Cultural Factors in Human Resource Management." *SHRM Research Quarterly* 19: 1–10.

Sperry, Len, and Maureen Duffy. 2009. "Workplace Mobbing: Family Dynamics and Therapeutic Considerations." *American Journal of Family Therapy* 37: 433–442.

Stillman, Richard J. 2010. "The Formal Structure: The Concept of Bureaucracy," in *Public Administration Concepts and Cases*, ed. Richard J. Stillman, 9th ed., 50–53. Boston: Wadsworth.

Susskind, Lawrence, and Patrick Field. 2012. "Dealing with an Angrier Public." *AC Resolution* 11, no. 3: 7–13.

Tannen, Deborah. 1990. *You Just Don't Understand: Women and Men in Conversation.* New York: William Morrow.

Taylor, Jeannette, and Ranald Taylor. 2010. "Working Hard for More Money or Working Hard to Make a Difference? Efficiency Wages, Public Service Motivation, and Effort." *Review of Public Personnel Administration* 31, no. 1: 68–86.

Thomas, Gail Fann, Roxanne Zolin, and Jackie L. Hartman. 2009. "The Central Role of Communication in Developing Trust and its Effect on Employee Involvement." *Journal of Business Communication* 46, no. 3: 287–310.

Thomson, Ann Marie, and James L. Perry. 2006. "Collaboration Processes: Inside the Black Box." *Public Administration Review* 66, no. S1: 20–32.

Ting-Toomey, Stella, and John G. Oetzel. 2001. *Managing Intercultural Conflict Effectively.* Thousand Oaks, CA: Sage.

Tracy, Sarah J., Jess K. Alberts, and Kendra Dyanne Rivera. 2007. *How to Bust the Office Bully: Eight Tactics for Explaining Workplace Abuse to Decision-Makers.* The Project for Wellness and Work-Life, Arizona State University.

Tracy, Sarah J., and Margaret Durfy. 2007. "Speaking Out in Public: Citizen Participation in Contentious School Board Meetings." *Discourse and Communication* 1, no. 2: 223–249.

Tracy, Sarah J., Pamela Lutgen-Sandvik, and Jess K. Alberts. 2006. "Nightmares,

Demons, and Slaves: Exploring the Painful Metaphors of Workplace Bullying." *Management Communication Quarterly* 20, no. 2: 148–185.

U.S. Bureau of Labor Statistics. 2010. "Table A-2. Employment Status of the Civilian Population by Race, Sex, and Age." Household Data, Labor Force Statistics, February 5. www.bls.gov/webapps/legacy/cpsatab2.htm.

U.S. Department of Transportation. 2013. *Public Involvement Techniques for Transportation Decision-Making.* www.fhwa.dot.gov/planning/public_involvement/publications/techniques/chapter00.cfm.

U.S. Office of Personnel Management. 2012. Senior Executive Service: Executive Core Qualifications. www.opm.gov/policy-data-oversight/senior-executive-service/executive-core-qualifications/.

Ury, William. 2007. *The Power of a Positive No: How to Say No and Still Get to Yes.* New York: Bantam.

Vandenabeele, Wouter. 2011. "Who Wants to Deliver Public Service? Do Institutional Antecedents of Public Service Motivation Provide an Answer?" *Review of Public Personnel Administration* 31, no. 1: 87–107.

Van Wart, Montgomery. 2003. "Public-Sector Leadership Theory: An Assessment." *Public Administration Review* 63, no. 2: 214–228.

———. 2011. *Dynamics of Leadership in Public Service: Theory and Practice.* 2d ed. Armonk, NY: M.E. Sharpe.

Vardi, Yoav, and Ely Weitz. 2004. *Misbehavior in Organizations: Theory, Research, and Management.* Mahwah, NJ: Lawrence Erlbaum.

Vigoda-Gadot, Eran, and Galit Meisler. 2010. "Emotions in Management and the Management of Emotions: The Impact of Emotional Intelligence and Organizational Politics on Public Sector Employees." *Public Administration Review* 270, no. 1: 72–86.

Walker, Polly O. 2004. "Decolonizing Conflict Resolution." *American Indian Quarterly* 28, nos. 3/4: 527–549.

Wang, Xiaohu. 2001. "Assessing Public Participation in U.S. Cities." *Public Performance & Management Review* 24, no. 4: 322–336.

Weber, Edward P., and Anne Khademian. 2008. "Wicked Problems, Knowledge Challenges, and Collaborative Capacity Builders in Network Settings." *Public Administration Review* 68, no. 2: 334–349.

Webster, Stephen C. 2009. "Singing Flashmob Highjacks Healthcare Conference." *The Raw Story*, October 24. www.rawstory.com/rs/2009/10/24/singing-flashmob-hijacks-health-insurance-conference/.

Weitzel, Sloan R. 2004. "Three Keys to Effective Feedback." In *The CCL Guide to Leadership in Action: How Managers and Organizations Can Improve the Practice of Leadership,* ed. Martin Wilcox and Stephen Rush, 110–118. San Francisco: Jossey-Bass.

The White House. 2011a. Establishing a Coordinated Government-Wide Initiative to Promote Diversity and Inclusion in the Federal Workforce. August 18. www.whitehouse.gov/the-press-office/2011/08/18/executive-order-establishing-coordinated-government-wide-initiative-prom.

———. 2011b. Executive Order 135S3. Establishing a Coordinated Governmentwide Initiative to Promote Diversity and Inclusion in the Federal Workforce. August 18. www.whitehouse.gov/the-press-office/2011/08/18/executive-order-establishing-coordinated-government-wide-initiative-prom.

Whitener, Ellen M. 2001. "Do 'High Commitment' Human Resource Practices Affect Employee Commitment? A Cross-Level Analysis Using Hierarchical Linear Modeling." *Journal of Management* 27: 515–535.

Witt, Stephanie. 2010. "Tips for Being an Effective Intergovernmental Collaborator." EzineArticles.com, March 9. http://ezinearticles.com/?Tips-For-Being-an-Effective-Intergovernmental-Collaborator&id=3885452.

Wong, Chi-Sum, and Kenneth S. Law. 2002. "The Effects of Leader and Follower Emotional Intelligence on Performance and Attitude: An Exploratory Study." *Leadership Quarterly* 13, no. 3: 242–274.

Wright, Bradley. E. 2001. "Public-Sector Work Motivation: A Review of the Current Literature and a Revised Conceptual Model." *Journal of Public Administration Research and Theory* 4: 559–586.

———. 2007. "Public Service and Motivation: Does Mission Matter?" *Public Administration Review* 67, no. 1: 54–64.

Yang, Kaifeng, and Anthony Kassekert. 2009. "Linking Management Reform with Employee Job Satisfaction: Evidence from Federal Agencies." *Journal of Public Administration Research and Theory* 20: 413–436.

Zapf, Dieter, and Claudia Gross. 2001. "Conflict Escalation and Coping with Workplace Bullying: A Replication and Extension." *European Journal of Work and Organizational Psychology* 10, no. 4: 497–522.

Zellars, Kelly L., Bennett J. Tepper, and Michelle K. Duffy. 2002. "Abusive Supervision and Subordinates' Organizational Citizenship Behavior." *Journal of Applied Psychology* 87, no. 6: 1068–1076.

Index

A

Accountability, 4, 6, 52, 69–70, 85, 95, 155, 173
Accusatory "you", 32, 36
Adaptive work, 7
Anger, 32, 33, 109
Apprentice stage, 26
Argumentativeness, 104, 109
Assertiveness, 59
Attribution errors, 15–17, 32–33, 47, 52
Audience analysis, 136–139
Avoidance, 40

B

Bad apples, 97
Boundaries, 107, 108
Brainstorming, 92–93
Broken record technique, 117
Bullying, 108–116
  bullying-up, 109
  responses, 113–116

C

Charrette, 162
Charismatic leaders, 60
Chilling effects, 157–158
Close-ended questions, 46

Closure, 15
Coaching, 69
Collaborative decision processes, 38, 161–162
Collaborative listening, 44
Collectivism, 125–127
Commitment, 64–65, 67, 88
Common goals, 36
Commonalities, 93
Communication
  channel, 18
  mechanical model, 18
  myths, 13–14
  nonverbal, 19
  noise, 18
  style, 38–40
Competition, 40
Conflict, 7–8, 28
  analysis, 49–55
  causes, 29–40, 49–50
  cost-effectiveness, 52
Connotative meaning, 19
Control issues, 107
Control systems, 67
Constituencies, 85
Credibility, 138–139, 151
Culture, 8–9, 16, 19, 31, 120–133
  conflict style, 129–131
  management styles, 132–133
  theory, 124–129

D

Decision methods, 93, 159
Decoding, 18
Defensiveness, 32, 36, 39, 40, 45, 76, 108
Demographics, 137–138
Demotivators, 62, 69, 72–77
Difficult people, 94, 103–109
Diversity, 8–9, 120–124

E

Employee morale, 22
Employee motivation, 4, 22, 60–69, 122
Employee recognition system, 62–63
Emotion, 35–36, 49
Emotional intelligence, 58–59, 67
Emotional labor, 59–60
Emotional paraphrasing, 44–45
Empathy, 59
Encoding, 18
Escalator style, 39–40
Essentializing, 124
Evidence, 140–141
Eye contact, 146–147

F

Face saving, 36
Fear, 105, 107
Federal Executive Service Standards, 9–12, 20, 21
Feedback, 66, 77–80
Figure/ground phenomenon, 14
Followership, 21

Four-step feedback, 78
Fractionator style, 39–40
Fugibility, 84
Future focus, 46

G

Generations, 72–73
Genuinely curious question, 33, 479–81
Goals, 66–69
Good natured banter, 36
Grievance procedures, 29
God and devil terms, 167
Ground rules, 94
Groups
  maintenance activities, 88, 91
  task activities, 88
Guest speaker management, 90, 153–154

H

Handouts, 149–150
High conflict individual, 108
High-low context cultures, 127–128, 131
Hofstede's cultural value dimensions, 128–129
Humor, 79

I

"I" language, 36, 117
Ideological constructs, 37
Incivility, 23, 33, 91, 156–168
In-group, 125–126
Indignation, 105

Individualism, 125–127
Information asymmetry, 34
Information-based conflict, 34–35, 50
Information sharing, 69–71
Interagency collaboration, 82–87
Intercultural conflict style, 129–131
Interests, 28, 44, 50–54, 107, 171
Interpersonal relationships, 33–34, 57–73
Interviews, 52–55

J

Job design, 63–64

L

Laissez faire management, 74
Leadership, 20–21, 82
 pitfalls, 21–26
Listening, 43–46, 171
 vs. hearing, 18

M

Managing expectations, 70, 159, 162–165
Mapping, 50–54, 109
Meeting management, 88–95
Message, 18
Message organization, 139–143
Metacommunication, 33
Miles' Law, 16
Mirroring technique, 54–55
Mixed message, 19
Mutual gains, 40, 50

N

Network of Schools of Public Policy, Affairs, and Administration (NASPAA), 9, 120
Networking, 5–6, 26
Neuroscience, 59
Norms, 96–97
Nature vs. nurture controversy, 16–18

O

Ombudsperson, 53
Open-ended questions, 44, 46–49, 53
Organizational citizenship, 21
Organizational culture, 20, 23

P

Parliamentary procedure, 98–102
Passive-aggressiveness, 22, 36, 40, 59, 91, 104
Pause gap, 17
Pay-for-performance, 62
Perception, 14–15, 17
Performance reviews, 65–69, 71, 133
Personal space, 128
Polychronic time, 128
Positions, 50–54
Positive homework, 46
Posters, 149–150
Postponement, 46
Power, 28, 29–33, 49, 174
 cultural views of, 128
 power balancing, 31

power struggles, 31, 37
traditional distributive, 30
PowerPoint presentations, 127–152
Probing questions, 47
Problem-solving process, 35, 37
Protected classes, 109–110
Pseudo-conflict, 43
Public meetings, 3, 155–168
Public service motivation, 61–62
Public speaking, 135–147
Public testimony, 148–149

R

Rapport vs. report style, 16–17
Reframe, 44, 94, 108, 109, 166
Rhetorical questions, 167
Respect issues, 107–108
Rights perspective, 28–29
Robert's Rules of Order, 98–101
Rubber band technique, 92

S

Sandwiching 77
Sarcasm, 22, 36, 109
Saying "No", 75–77
Self-awareness, 58
Self-serving bias, 15
Sexual harassment, 109
Speaking notes, 144–145
Speech delivery, 144–147
Spiral of negativity, 31

Structural conflict, 36–37, 50
Style-based conflict, 38–40

T

Task-based conflict, 34, 49
Teams, 95–98
Threats, 79, 110
Training, 64, 69
Transformational leadership, 20
Transactional leadership, 20
Transparency, 4, 84, 159
Trust, 21, 31, 64–65, 66, 87

V

Values, 37–38, 50
Venting session, 161
Verbal aggressiveness, 36, 69, 103–109, 110
Visual aids, 147–152
Vocalized pause, 146

W

Weakness trap, 69
Weber, Max, 30
Wicked problems, 7
Work sequencing, 72
Workplace climate, 106
Workplace respect policies, 38, 50, 108

About the Authors

Suzanne McCorkle directs the Dispute Resolution academic programs and is a professor in the public policy and administration department at Boise State University. She formerly served as Associate Dean and Dean of the College of Social Sciences and Public Affairs. Dr. McCorkle is the author of *Mediation Theory and Practice* (2005) and *Personal Conflict Management* (2010) (both with Melanie Reese). Her consulting and research interests involve workplace conflict and its remedies.

Stephanie L. Witt is a professor of public policy and administration at Boise State University. Her books include *Cities, Sagebrush, and Solitude* (co-edited with Dennis Judd) and *Urban West Revisited: Governing Cities in Uncertain Times* (with James B. Weatherby). She has previously held positions at Boise State as Associate Vice President, Associate Dean, Department Chair and Director of the Public Policy Center. She is a Carnegie Foundation for the Advancement of Teaching "Idaho Professor of the Year" (1998).